EASY PIANO

CONTEMPORARY LOVE SONGS
FOR EASY PIANO

ISBN 0-634-02034-X

HAL•LEONARD®
CORPORATION

7777 W. BLUEMOUND RD. P.O. BOX 13819 MILWAUKEE, WI 53213

Visit Hal Leonard Online at
www.halleonard.com

BEAUTY AND THE BEAST
from Walt Disney's BEAUTY AND THE BEAST

Lyrics by HOWARD ASHMAN
Music by ALAN MENKEN

4

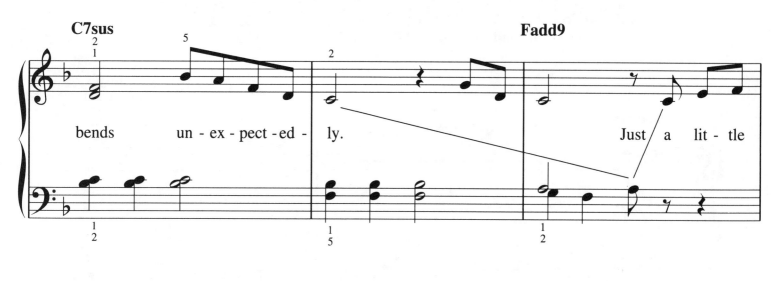

bends   un - ex - pect - ed -   ly.   Just a lit - tle

change.   Small, to say the   least.   Both a lit - tle

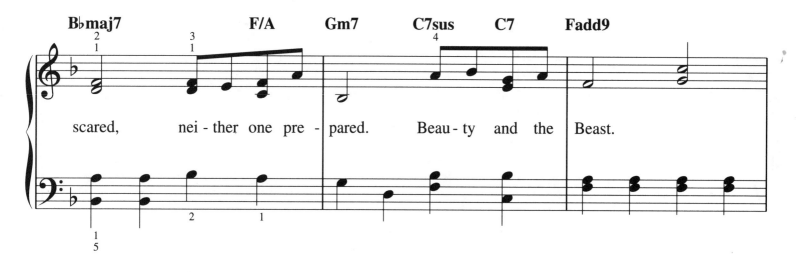

scared,   nei - ther one pre - pared.   Beau - ty and the   Beast.

Ev - er just the   same.   Ev - er a sur -

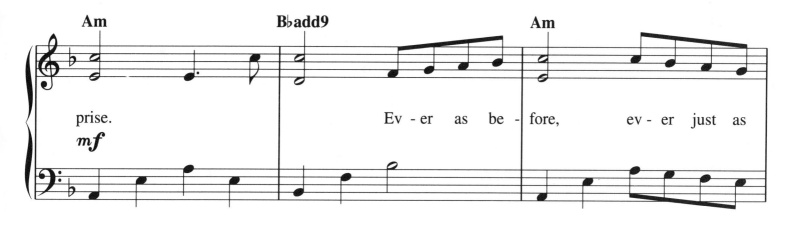

Am / B♭add9 / Am

prise. *mf*
Ev - er as be - fore, ev - er just as

Dm7 / E♭ / G / C

sure as the sun will rise. Tale as old as

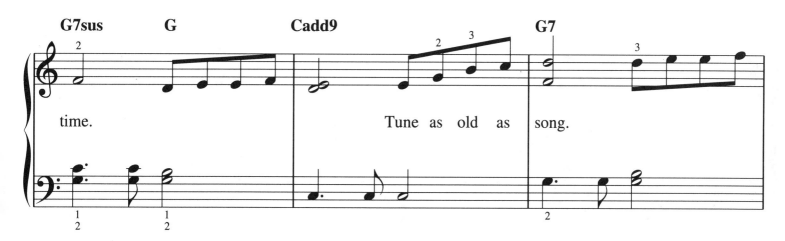

G7sus / G / Cadd9 / G7

time. Tune as old as song.

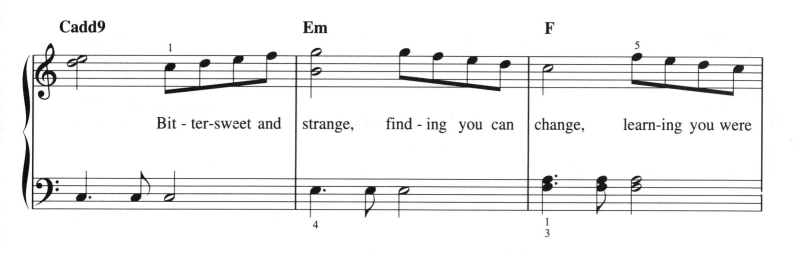

Cadd9 / Em / F

Bit - ter-sweet and strange, find - ing you can change, learn-ing you were

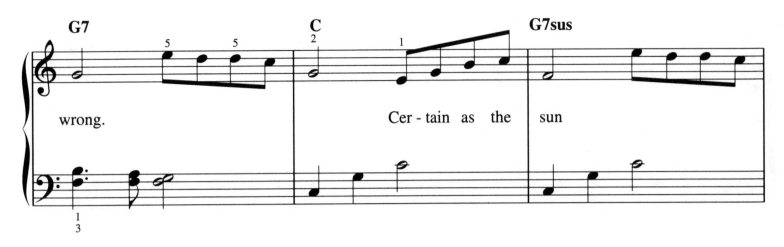

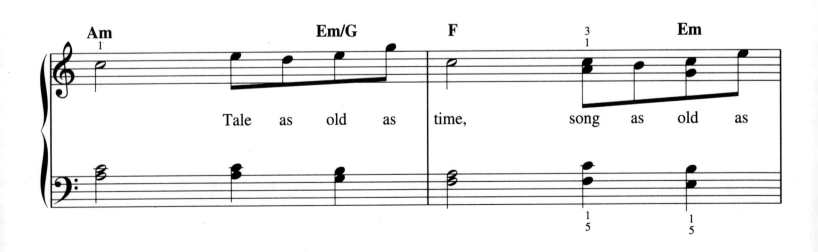

rhyme. Beau - ty and the Beast.

BREATHE

Words and Music by HOLLY LAMAR
and STEPHANIE BENTLEY

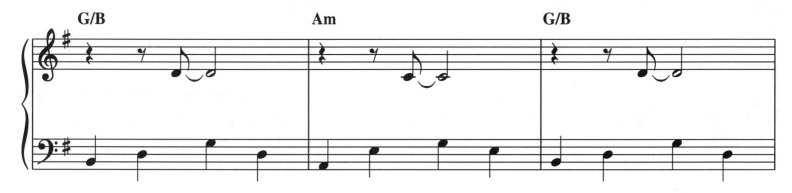

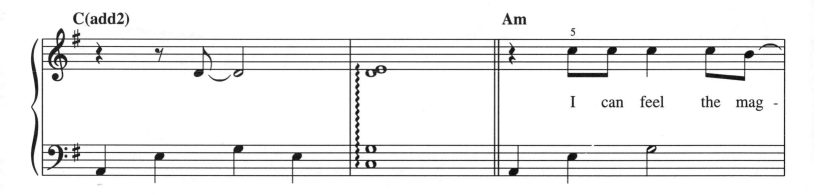

I can feel the mag-

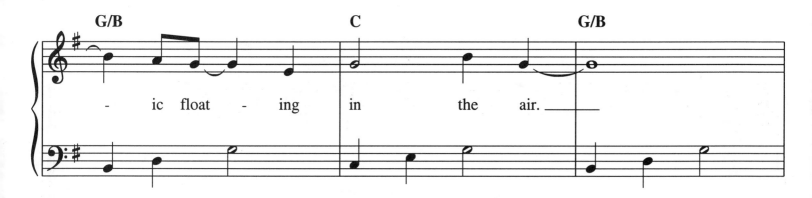

-ic float-ing in the air.

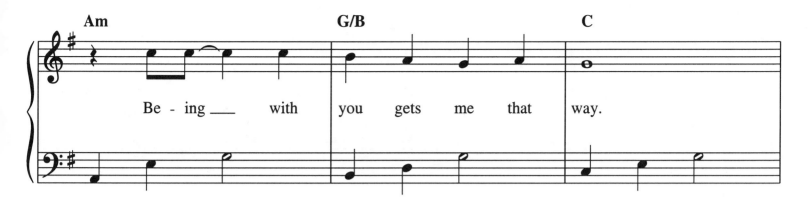

Be - ing ___ with you gets me that way.

I watch the sun - light dance a - cross ___

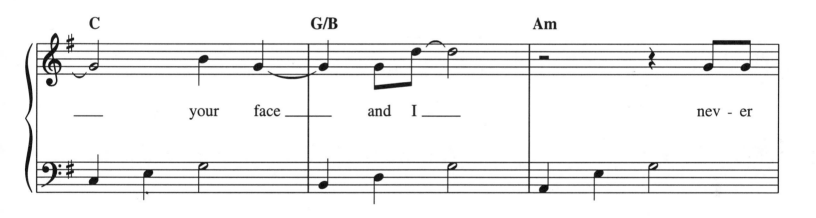

___ your face ___ and I ___ nev - er

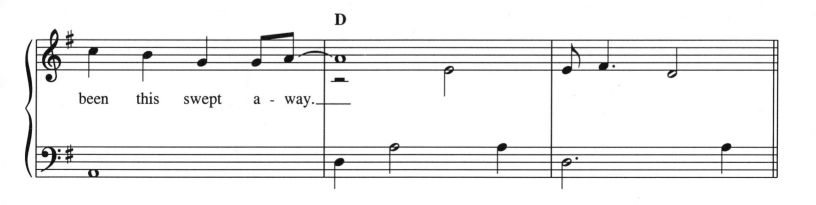

been this swept a - way. ___

All my thoughts just seem to set - tle on the breeze __
In a way I know my heart __ is wak - ing up __

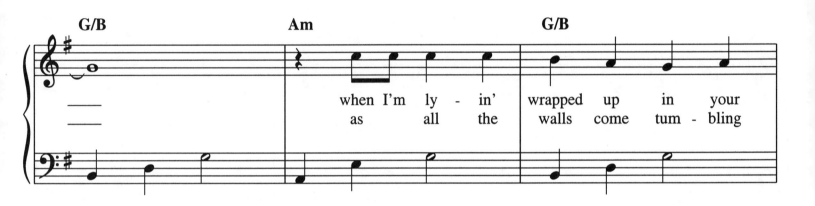

__ when I'm ly - in' wrapped up in your
__ as all the walls come tum - bling

arms. The whole world just
down. Clos-er than I've

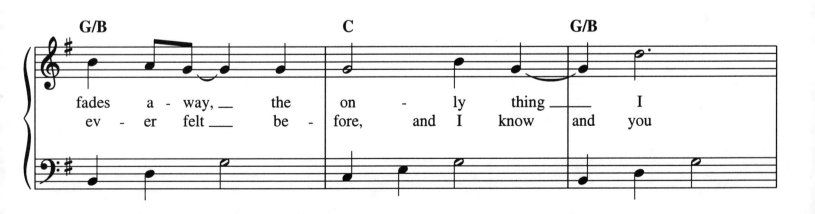

fades a - way, __ the on - ly thing __ I
ev - er felt __ be - fore, and I know and you

hear ..... is the beat - ing of ____ your heart.
know ..... there's no need for words _ right now.

'Cause I can feel you breathe, it's wash-ing o - ver me, and sud-den-ly I'm

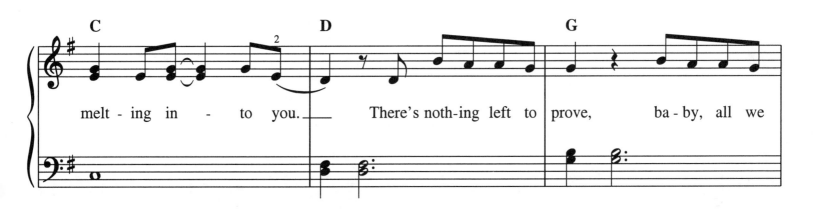

melt - ing in - to you. ____ There's noth-ing left to prove, ba - by, all we

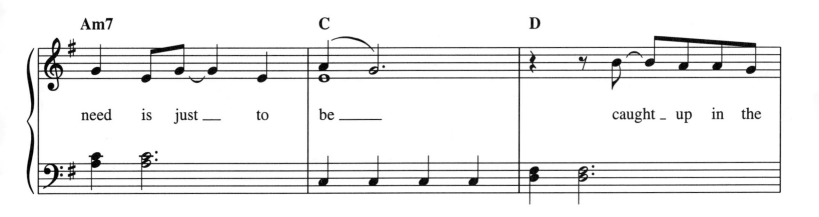

need is just ___ to be _____ caught _ up in the

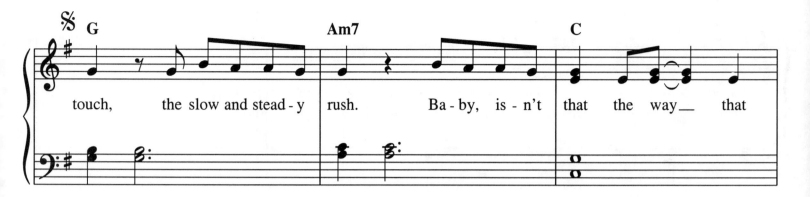

touch, the slow and stead-y rush. Ba-by, is-n't that the way_ that

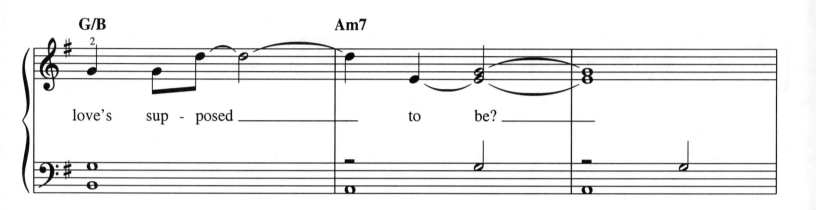

love's sup-posed _____ to be? _____

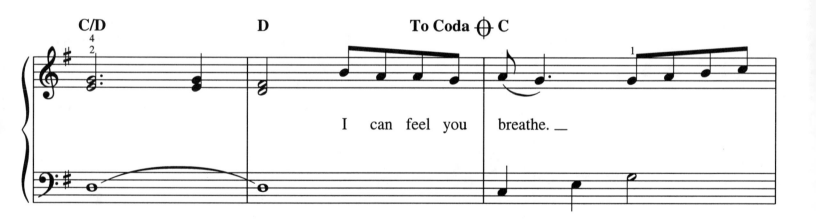

I can feel you breathe. _

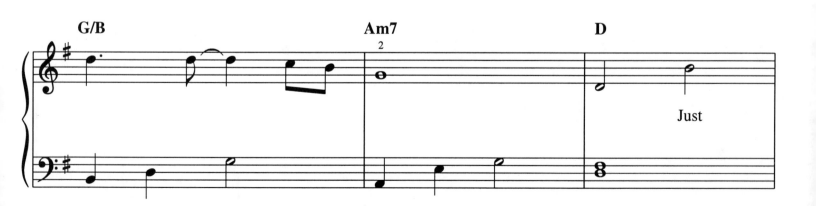

Just

breathe.

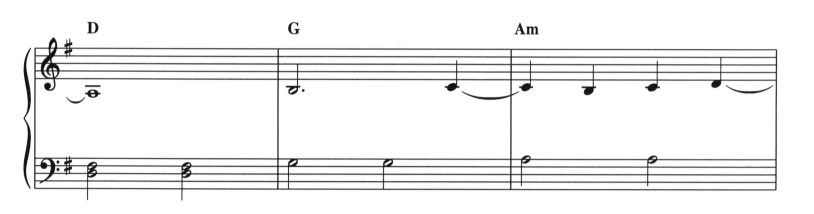

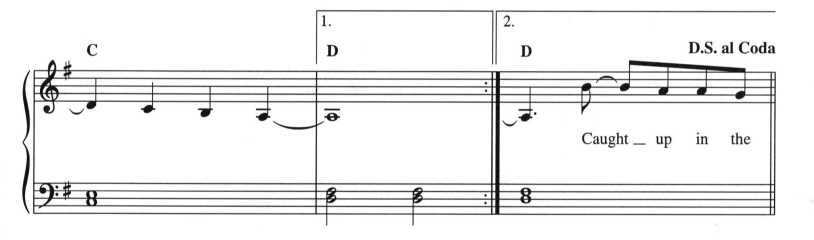

D.S. al Coda

Caught __ up in the

CODA

breathe. __

14

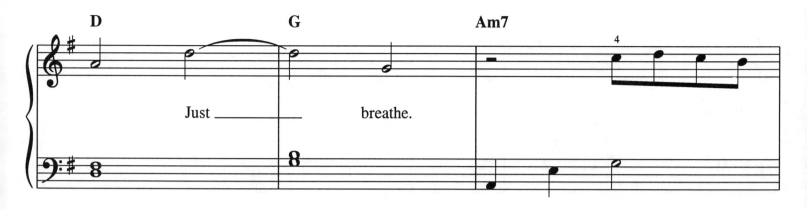

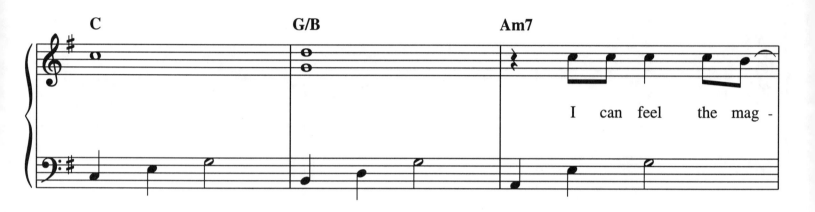

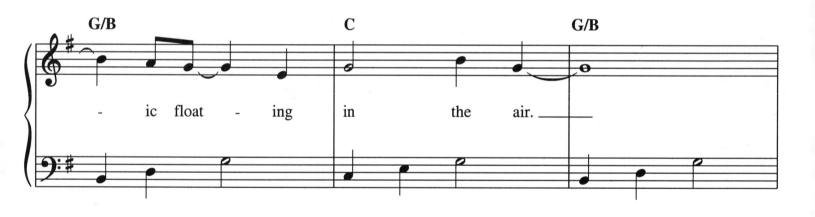

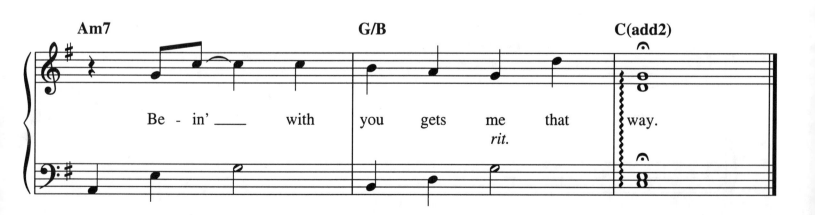

FOREVER AND EVER, AMEN

Words and Music by PAUL OVERSTREET
and DON SCHLITZ

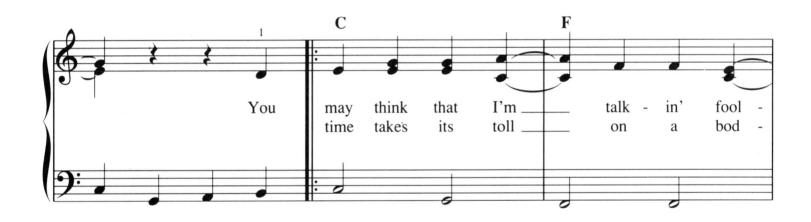

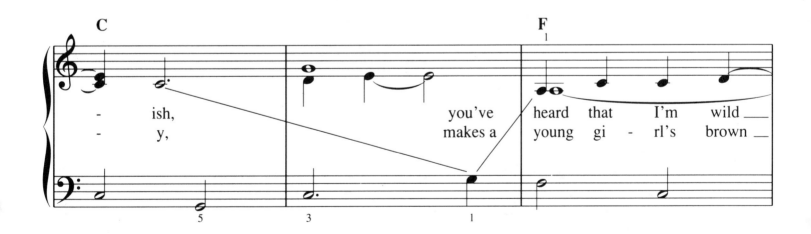

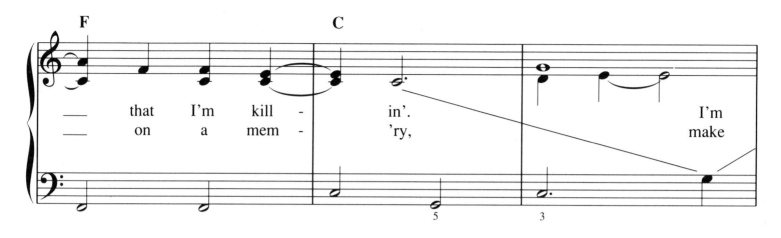

that I'm kill - in'. I'm
on a mem - 'ry, make

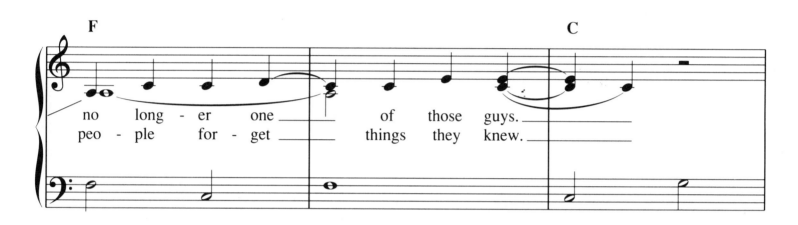

no long - er one of those guys.
peo - ple for - get things they knew.

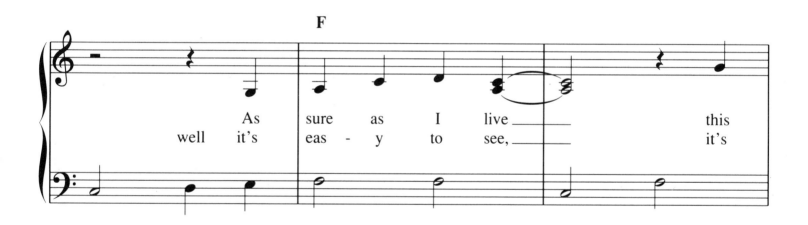

As sure as I live this
well it's eas - y to see, it's

love that I give is gon - na be yours
happen - in' to me. I've al - read - y for - got -

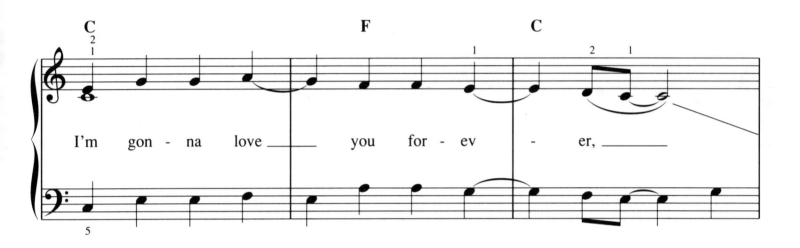

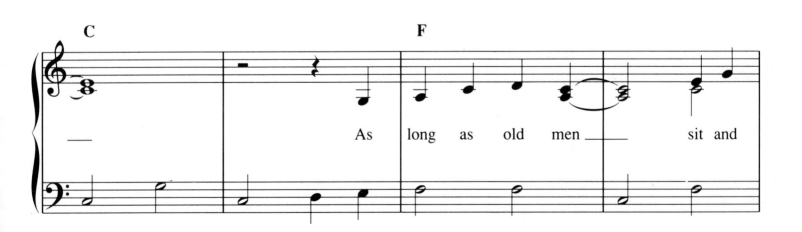

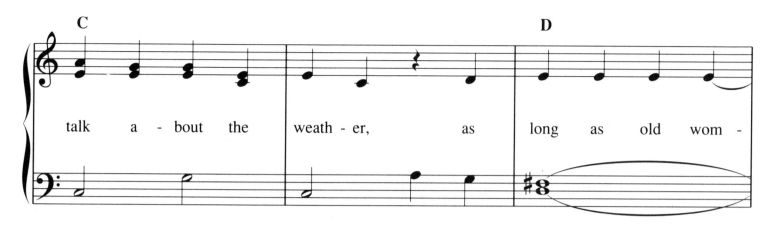

talk a - bout the weath - er, as long as old wom -

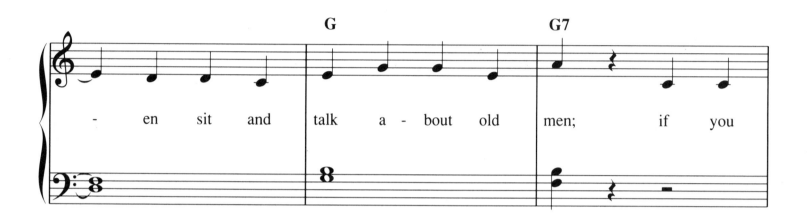

- en sit and talk a - bout old men; if you

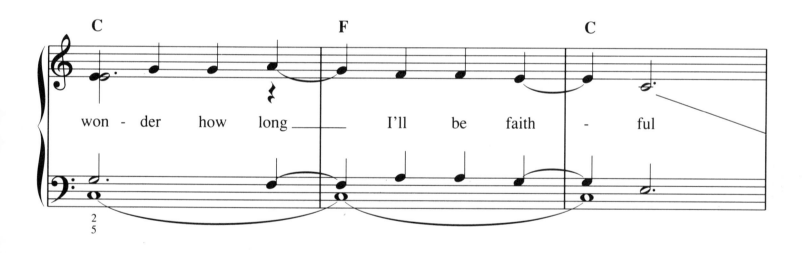

won - der how long _____ I'll be faith - ful

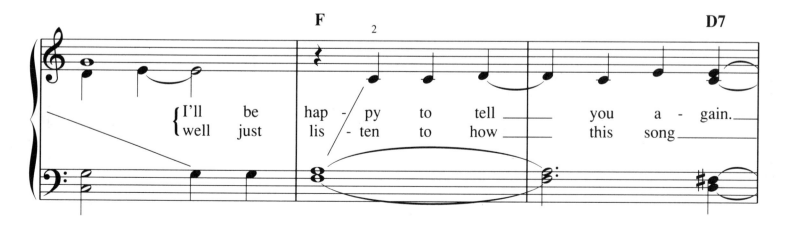

I'll be / well just

hap - / py to tell _____ you a - gain. lis / - ten to how _____ this song _____

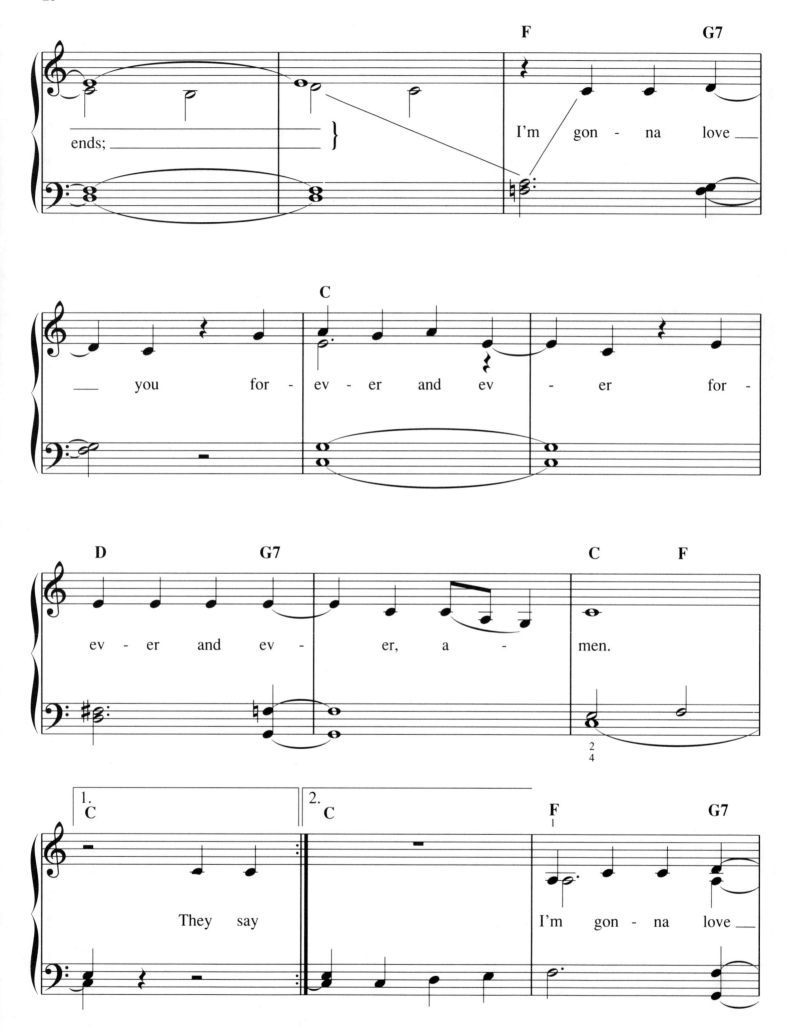

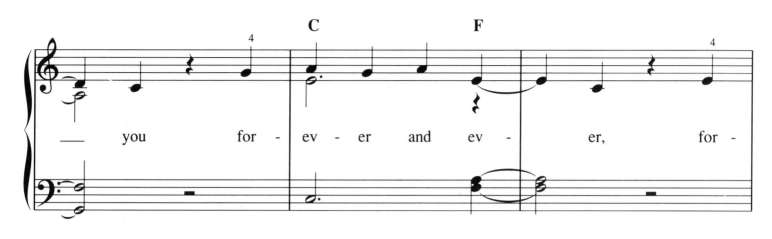

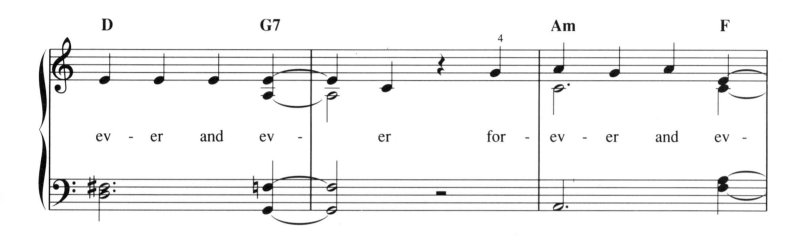

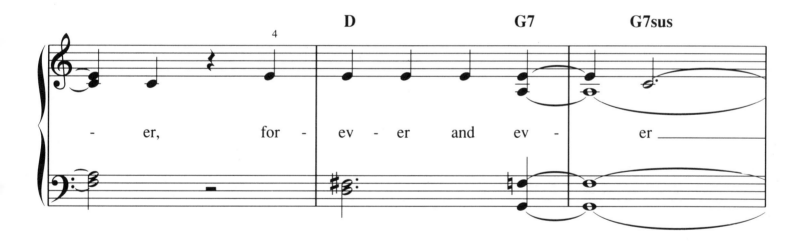

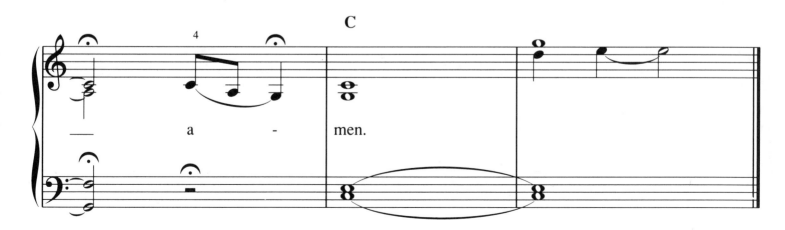

FOREVER IN LOVE

By KENNY G

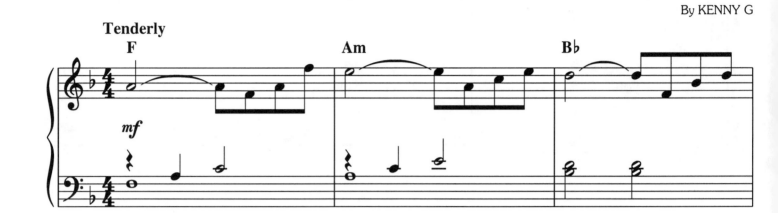

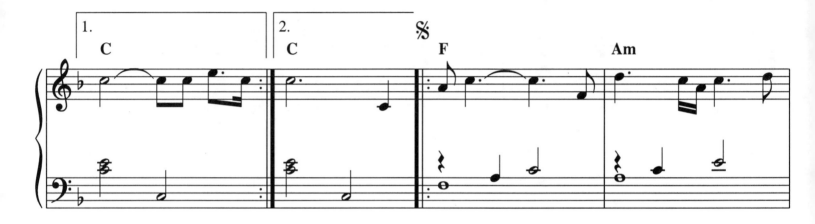

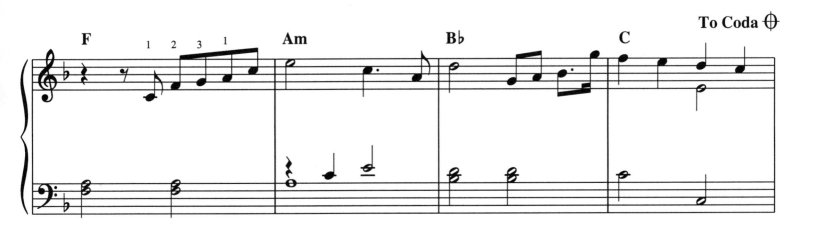

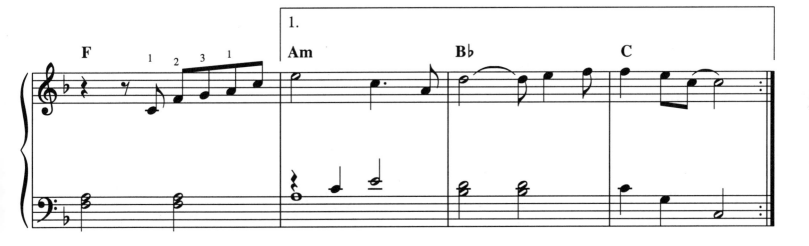

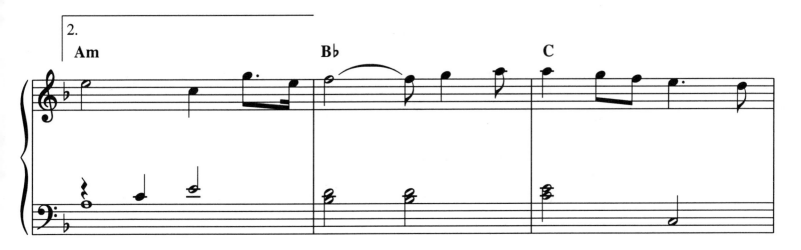

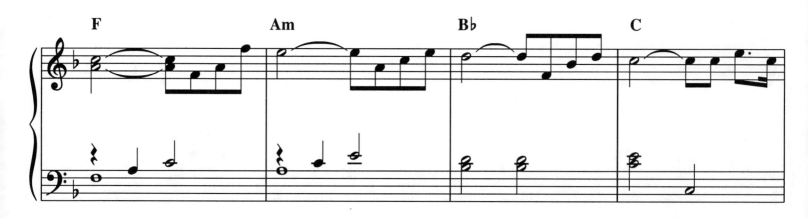

D.S. al Coda

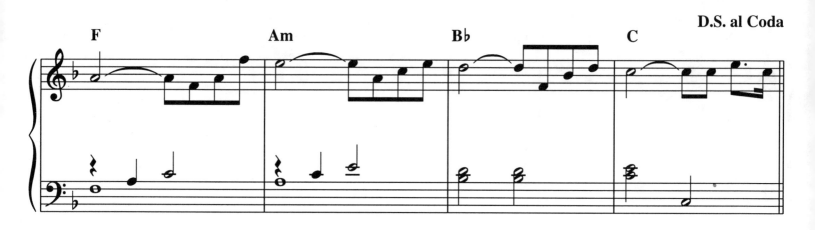

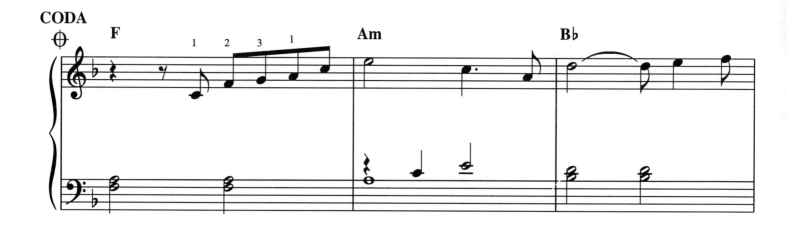

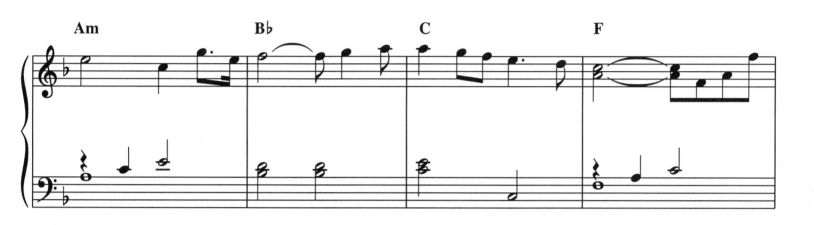

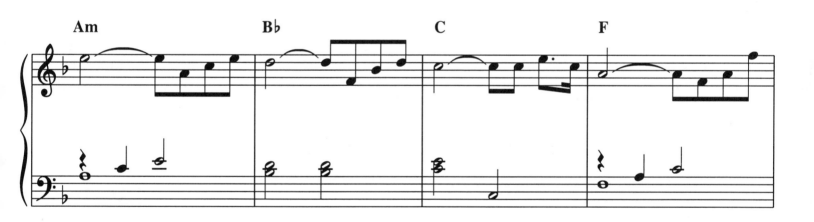

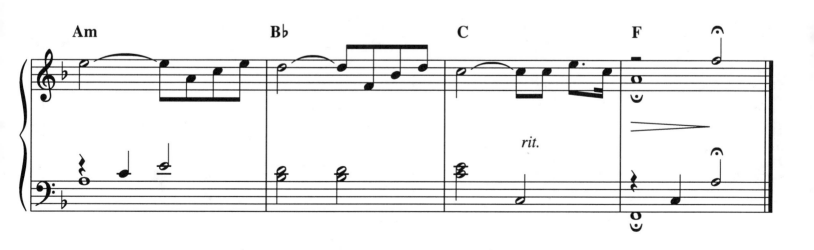

HERE AND NOW

Words and Music by TERRY STEELE
and DAVID ELLIOT

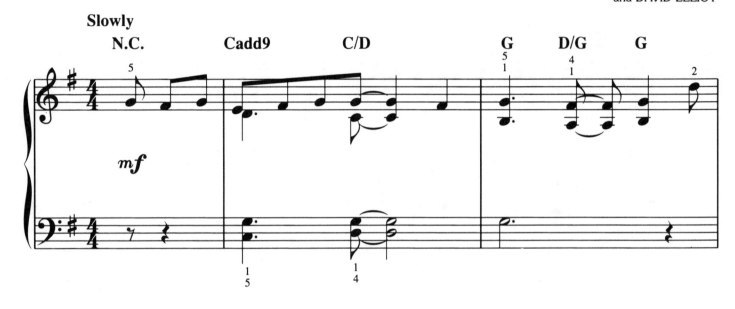

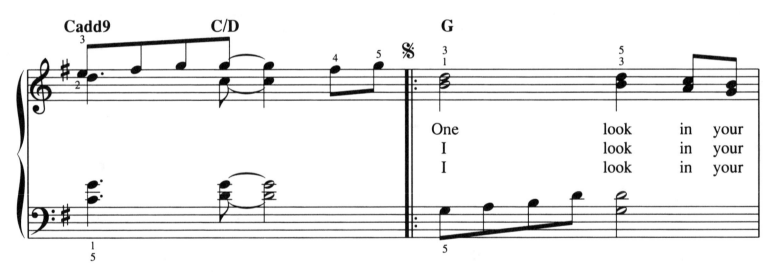

One look in your
I look in your
I look in your

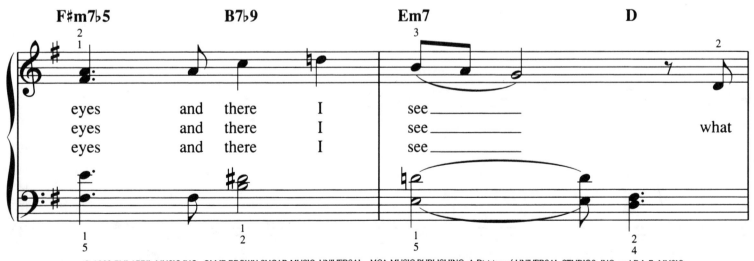

eyes and there I see _____
eyes and there I see _____
eyes and there I see _____ what

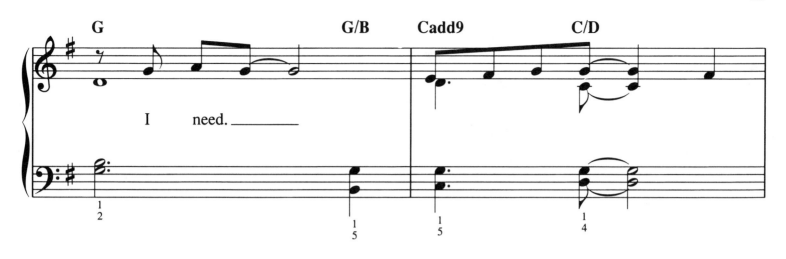

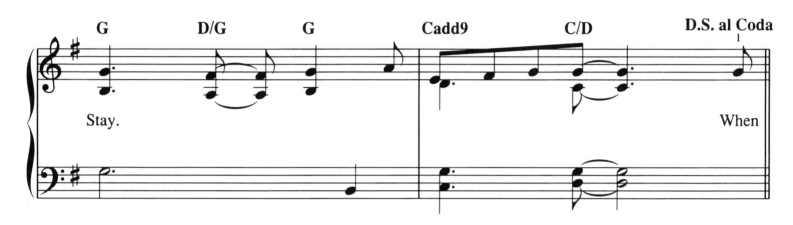

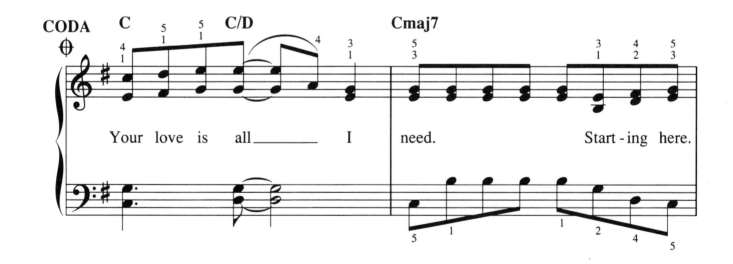

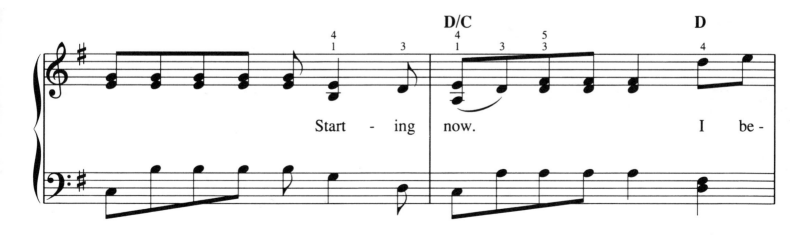

need. _____ Here and now I vow to be one _ with _

thee. _____ Your love is all I

need. Ay,

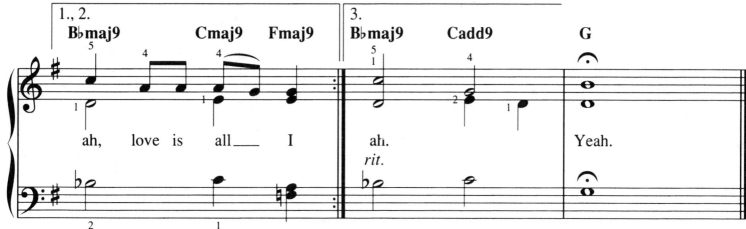

ah, love is all ___ I ah. Yeah.

rit.

I WANNA LOVE YOU FOREVER

Words and Music by SAM WATTERS
and LOUIS BIANCANIELLO

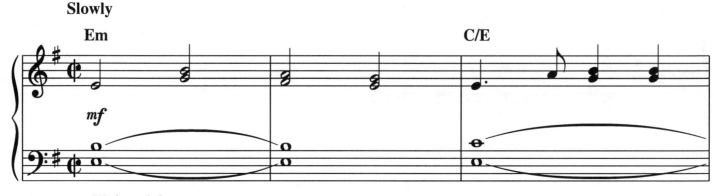

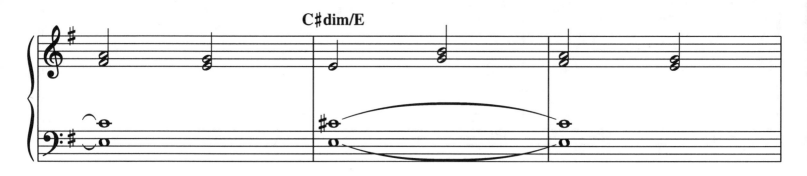

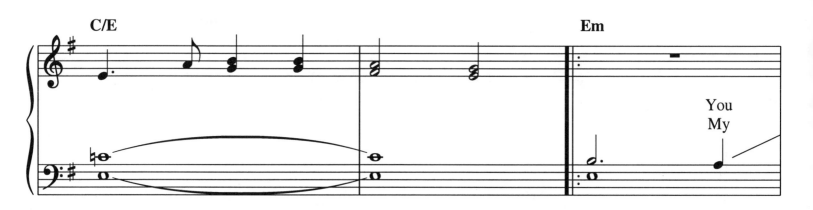

You
My

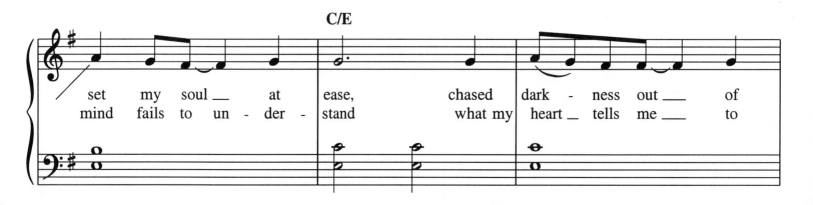

set my soul ___ at ease, chased dark - ness out ___ of
mind fails to un - der - stand what my heart ___ tells me ___ to

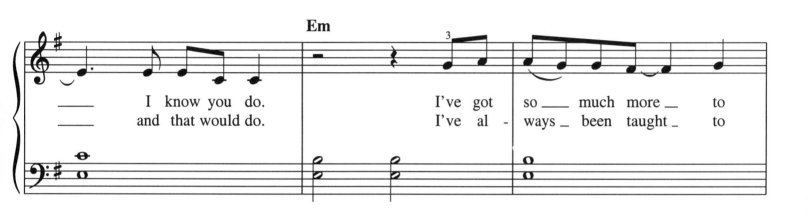

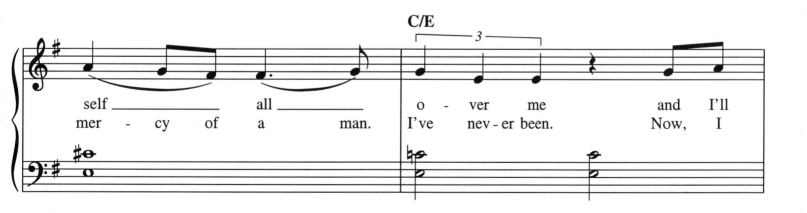

cher - ish ev - 'ry drop here on my knees.
on - ly want to be right where you are.
I wan - na

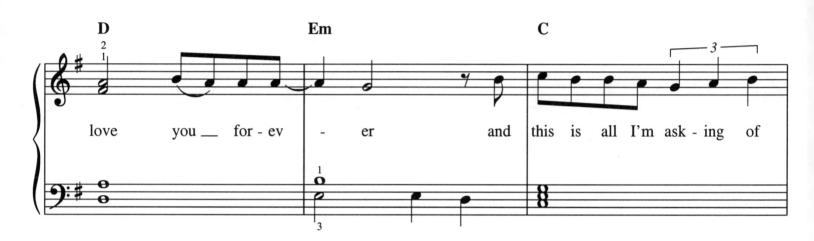

love you __ for - ev - er and this is all I'm ask - ing of

you. Ten thou - sand life - times __ to - geth - er, is

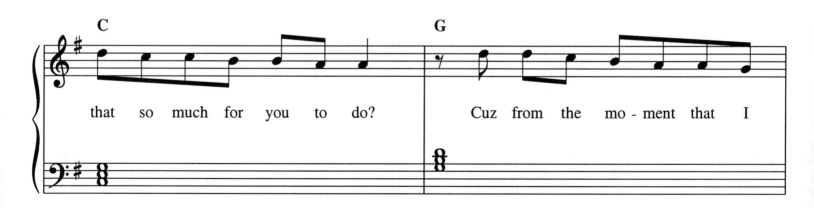

that so much for you to do? Cuz from the mo - ment that I

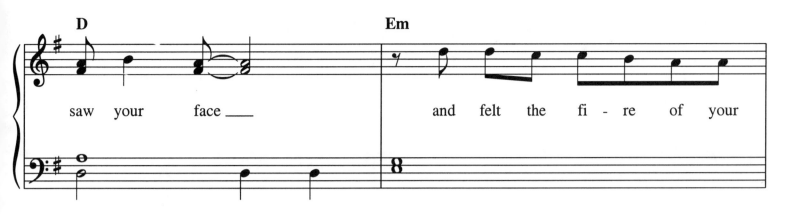

saw your face ___   and felt the fi - re of your

sweet em - brace, __ I swear I   know,   I'm gon - na ___ love   you   for - ev -

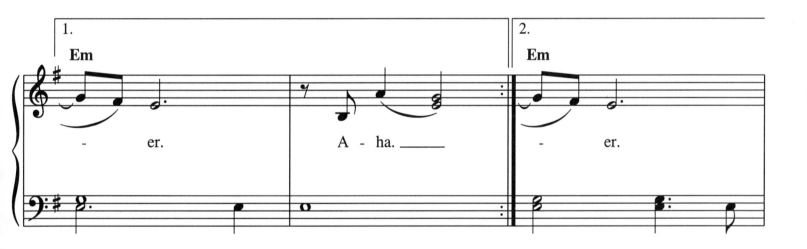

    - er.   A - ha. _____   - er.

Whoa, ___ oh, oh.   In my life I've learned that heav - en nev - er

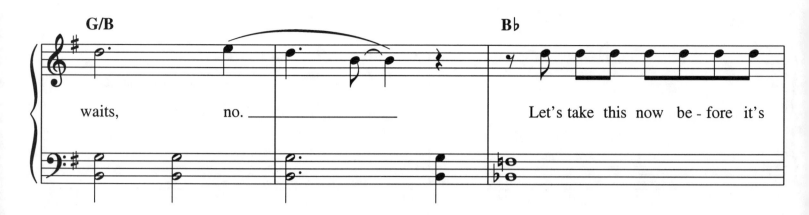

waits, no. _____ Let's take this now be-fore it's

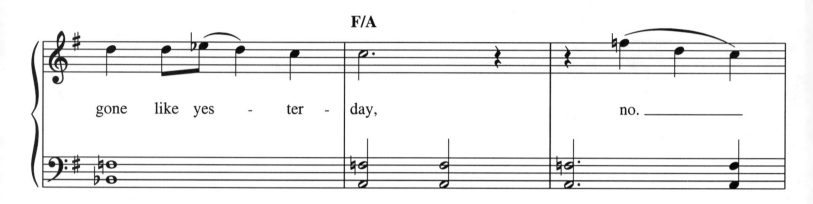

gone like yes - ter - day, no. _____

Cuz when I'm with you there's no - where else that I would ev - er

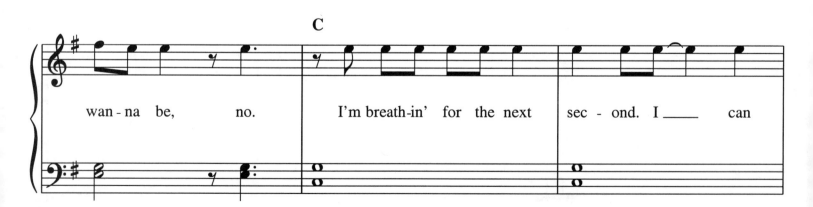

wan - na be, no. I'm breath-in' for the next sec - ond. I ___ can

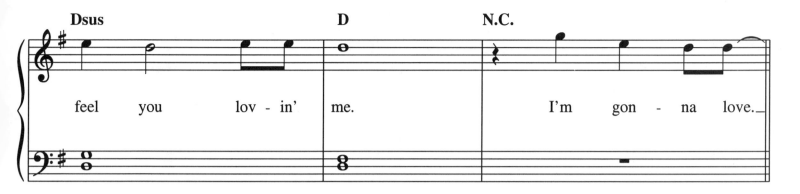

feel you lov - in' me. I'm gon - na love.

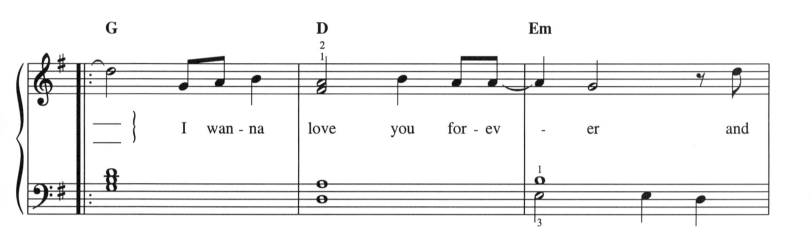

I wan - na love you for - ev - er and

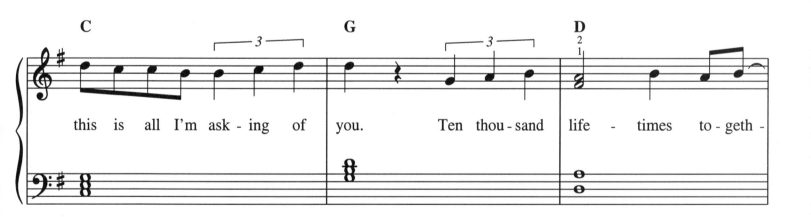

this is all I'm ask - ing of you. Ten thou - sand life - times to - geth -

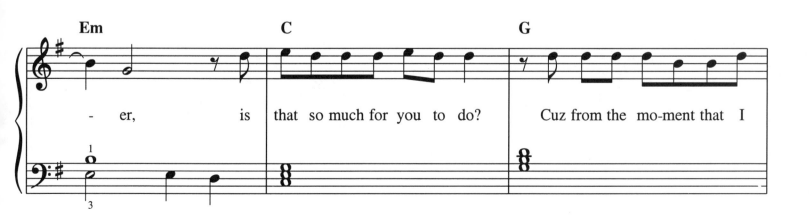

- er, is that so much for you to do? Cuz from the mo-ment that I

saw your face — and felt the fi - re of your

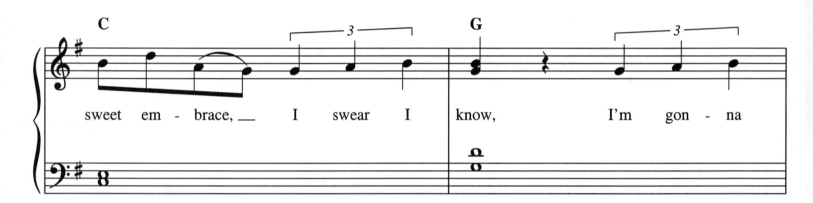

sweet em - brace, __ I swear I know, I'm gon - na

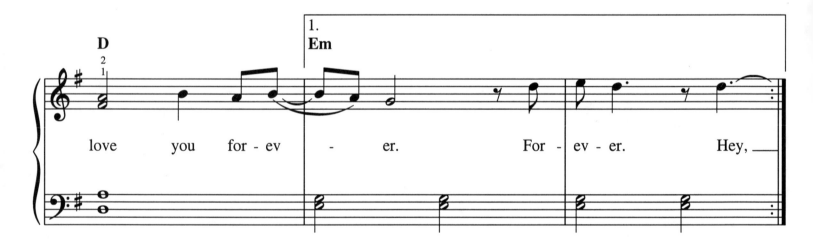

love you for - ev - er. For - ev - er. Hey, __

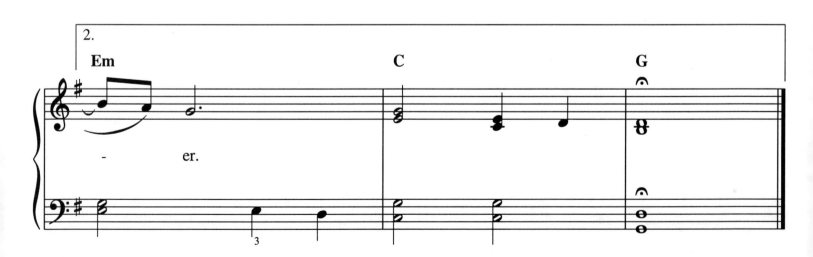

- er.

I WILL REMEMBER YOU

Theme from THE BROTHERS McMULLEN

Words and Music by SARAH McLACHLAN,
SEAMUS EGAN and DAVE MERENDA

42

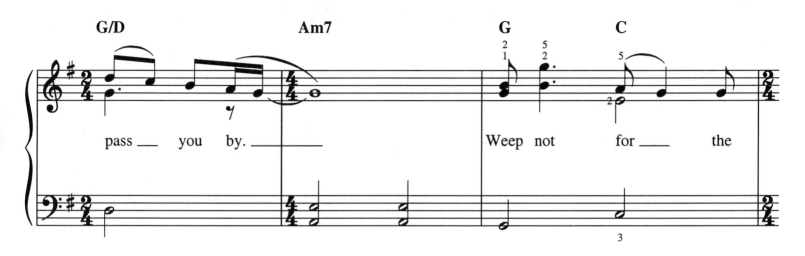

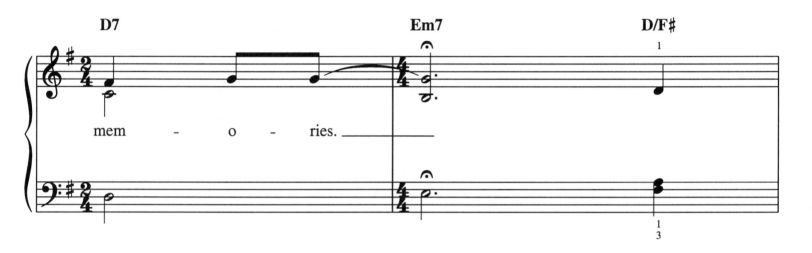

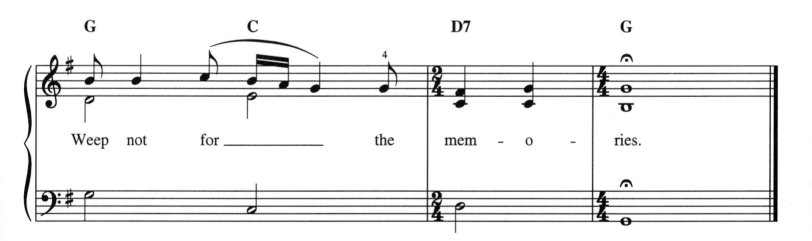

Additional Lyrics

3. I'm so afraid to love you, more afraid to lose,
   Clinging to a past that doesn't let me choose.
   Well, once there was a darkness, a deep and endless night.
   You gave me ev'rything you had, oh, you gave me light.

I WILL BE HERE FOR YOU

Words and Music by MICHAEL W. SMITH
and DIANE WARREN

Moderate Rock Ballad

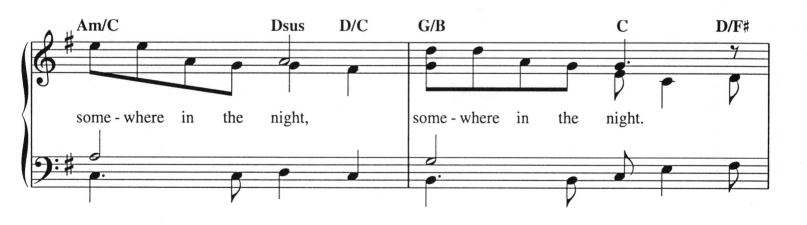

I'LL BE

Words and Music by
EDWIN McCAIN

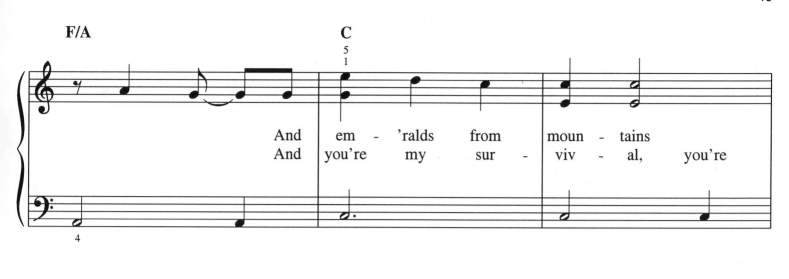

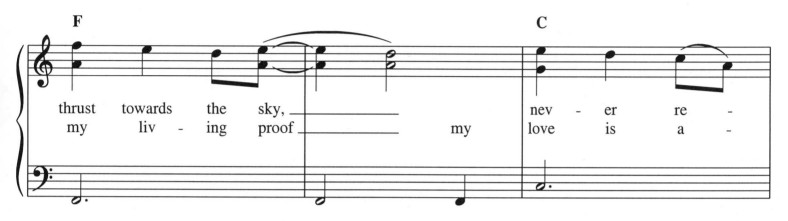

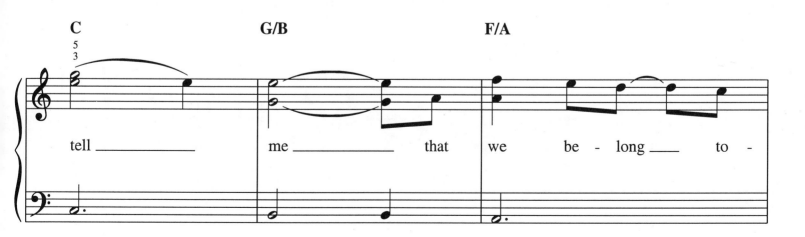

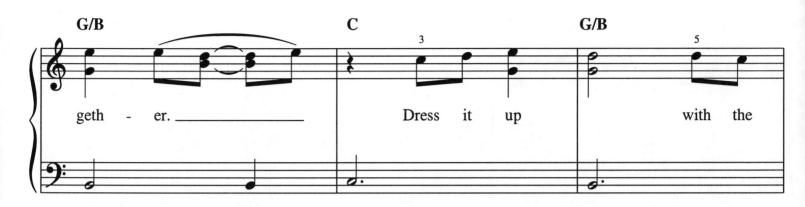

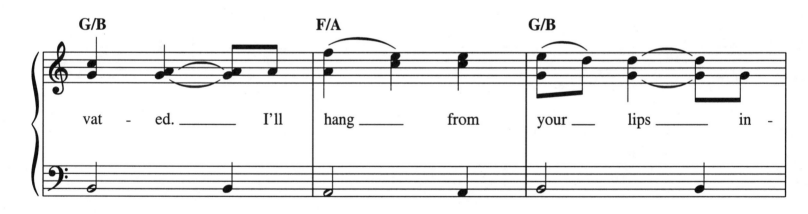

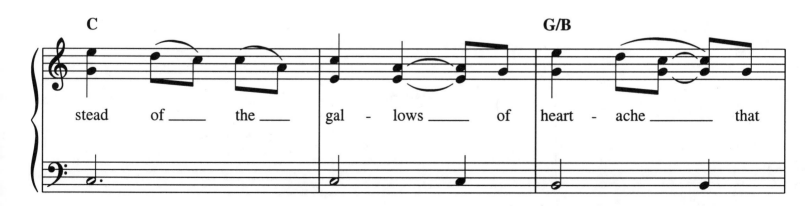

hang from a - bove.

I'll

be your cry - in' shoul - der, _____

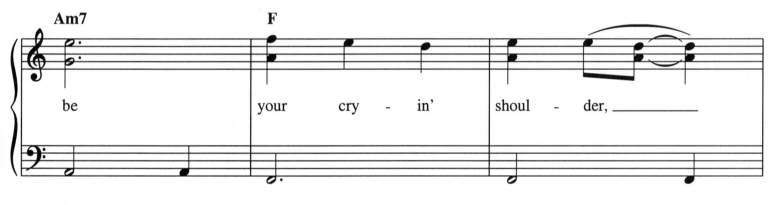

I'll _____ be _____ love su - i - cide. _____

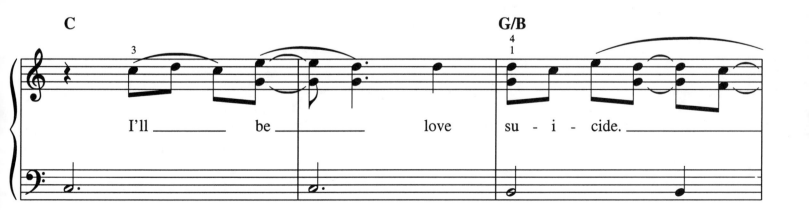

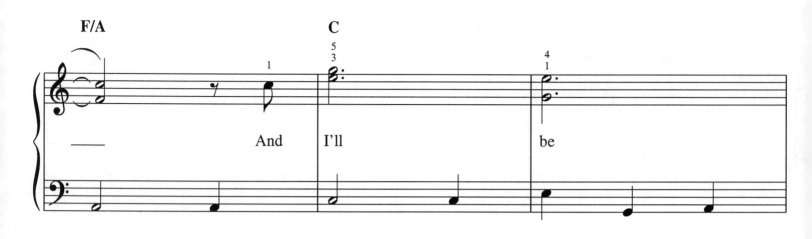

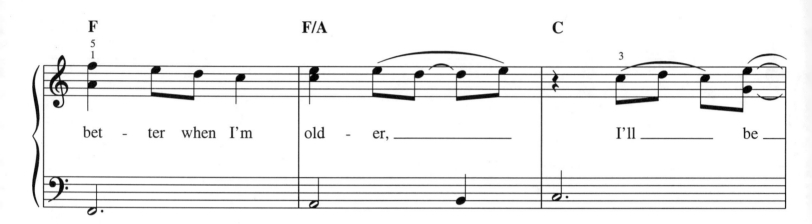

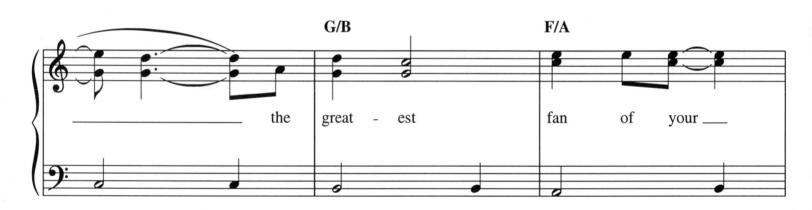

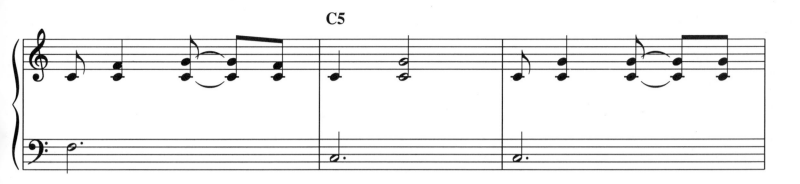

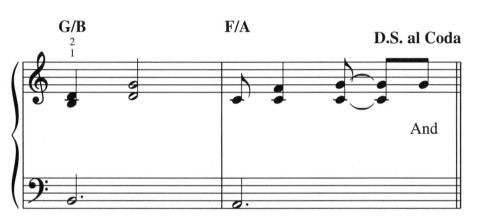

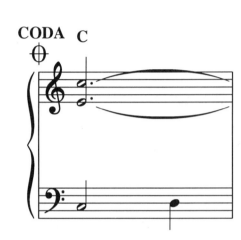

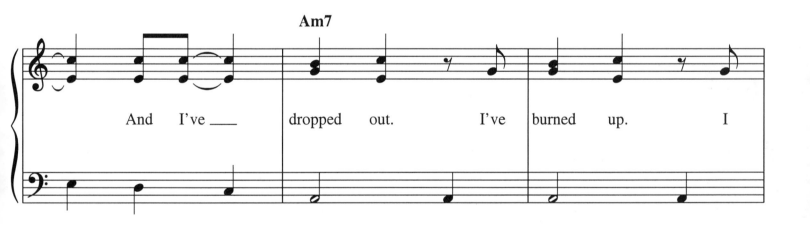

And I've ___ dropped out. I've burned up. I

fought my way back from the dead.___

54

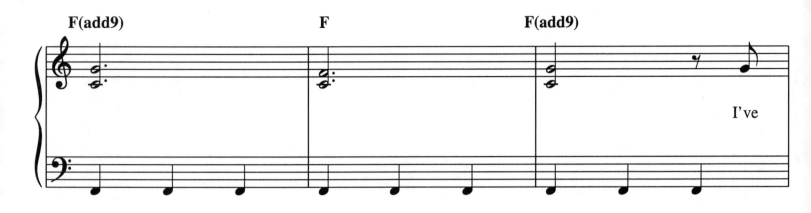

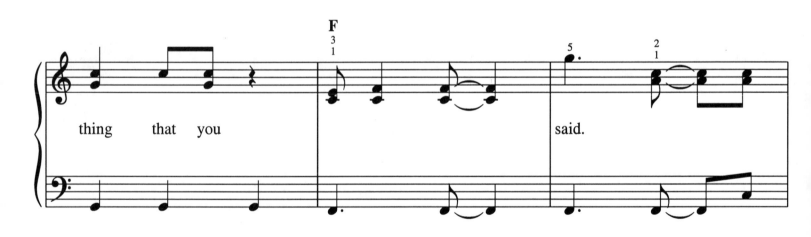

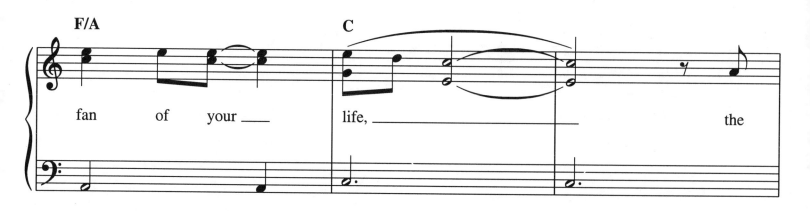

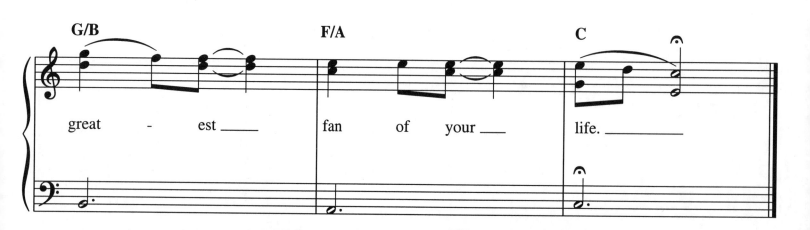

IT'S YOUR LOVE

Words and Music by
STEPHONY E. SMITH

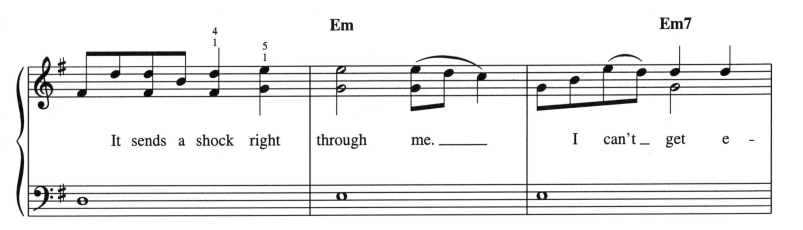

It sends a shock right through me. _____ I can't _ get e -

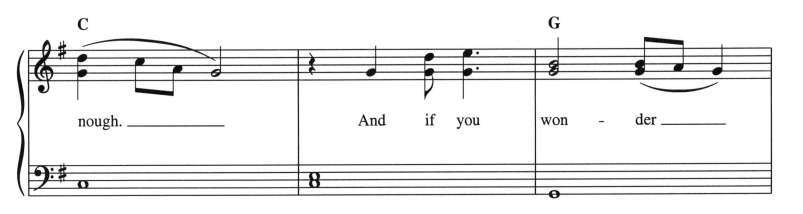

nough. _____ And if you won - der _____

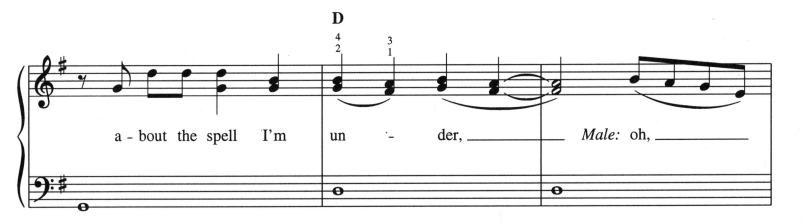

a - bout the spell I'm un - der, _____ *Male:* oh, _____

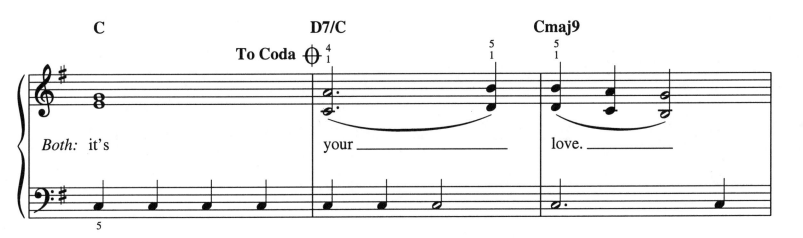

Both: it's your _____ love. _____

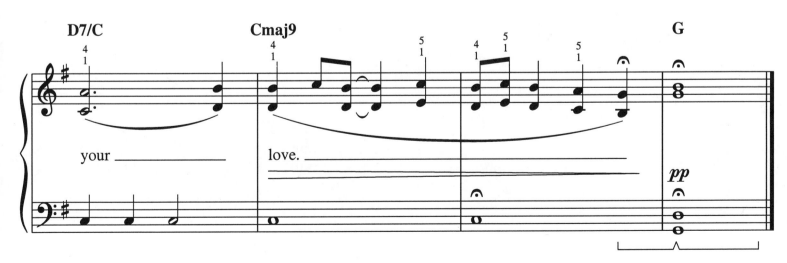

JUST THE WAY YOU ARE

Words and Music by
BILLY JOEL

Don't go / Don't go / said I — chang-ing / try - ing / love you — — to try and / some new / and that's for

please me. — / fash- ion. — / ev - er. — — You nev - er / Don't change the / And this I — let me down — be - / col - or of — your / prom - ise from — the

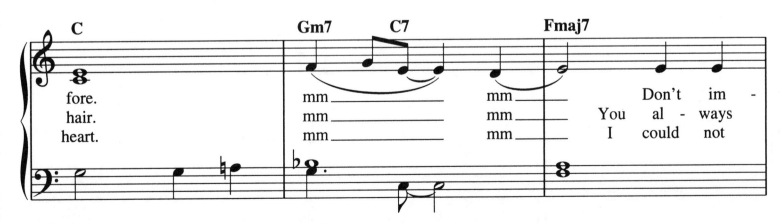

fore. / hair. / heart. — mm — mm — mm — — mm — mm — mm — — Don't im - / You al - ways / I could not

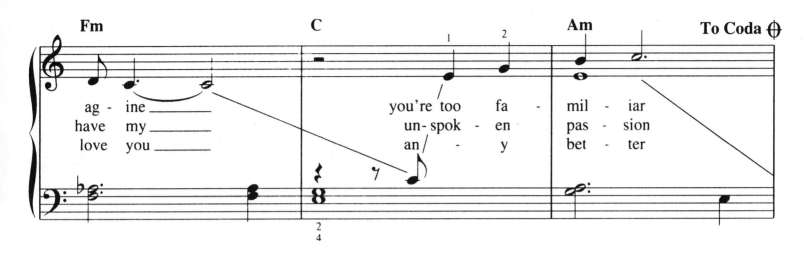

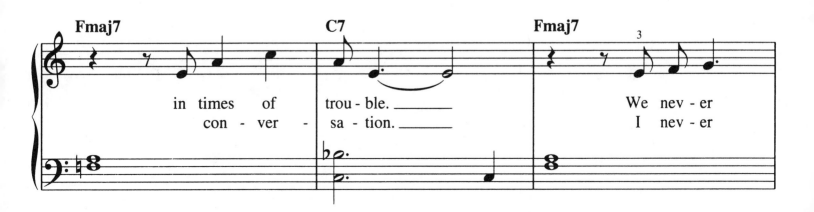

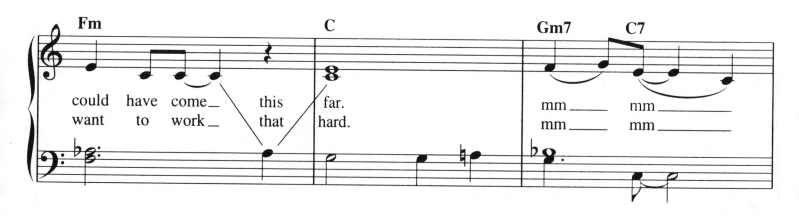

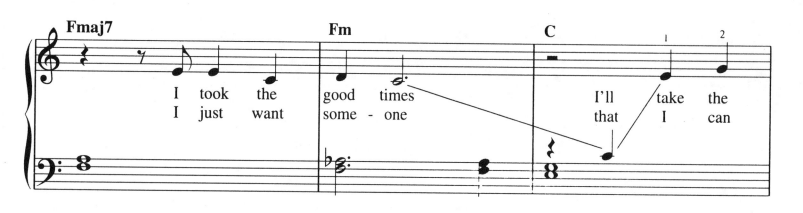

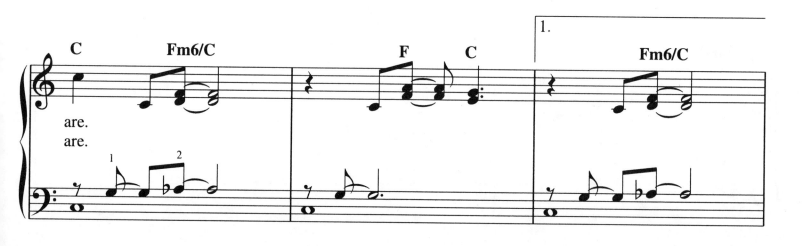

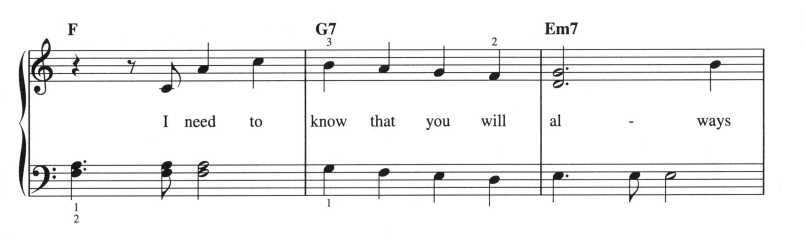

I need to know that you will al - ways

be. The same old some - one that I

knew. Oh! What will it

take till you be - lieve in me

The way that I be - lieve in you.

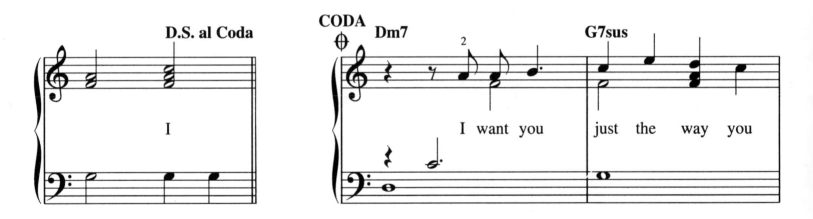

D.S. al Coda

I

CODA

Dm7

G7sus

I want you just the way you

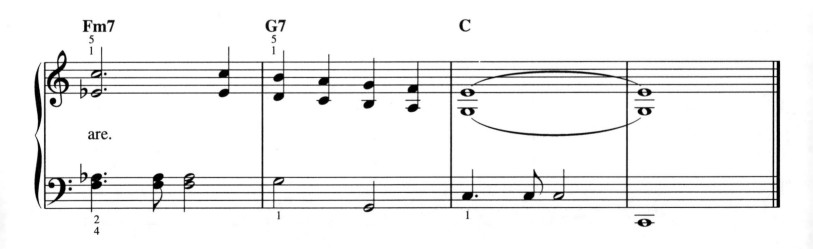

are.

SAVE THE BEST FOR LAST

Words and Music by PHIL GALDSTON,
JON LIND and WENDY WALDMAN

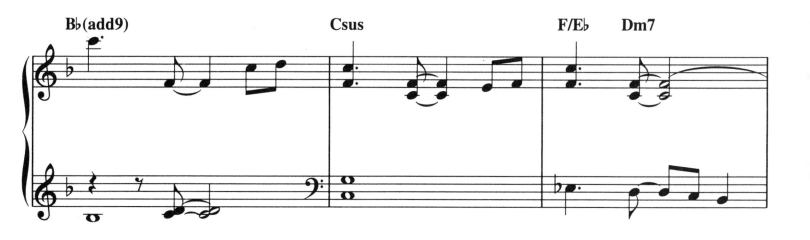

Some-times the | snow comes down_ in June. Some-times the
nights you came_ to me when some sil - ly
snow comes down_ in June. Some-times the

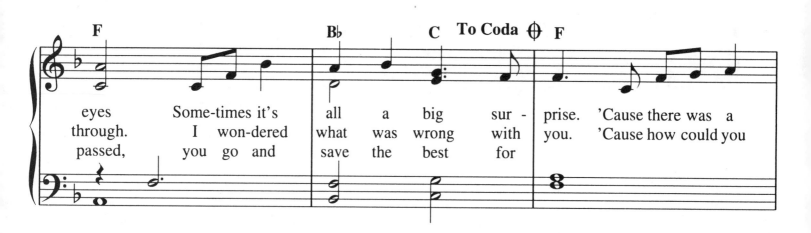

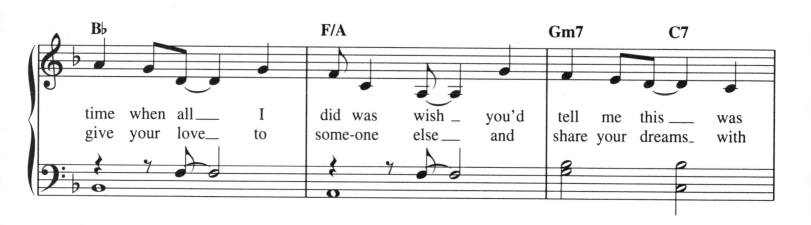

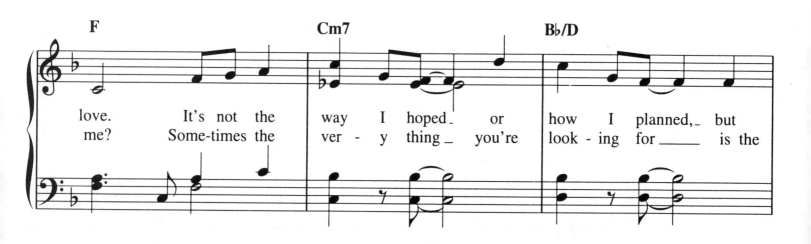

some - how it's e - nough. And now we're stand - ing face __ to
one thing you can't see. But now we're stand - ing face __ to

face.
face. Is - n't this world a cra - zy place? Just when I

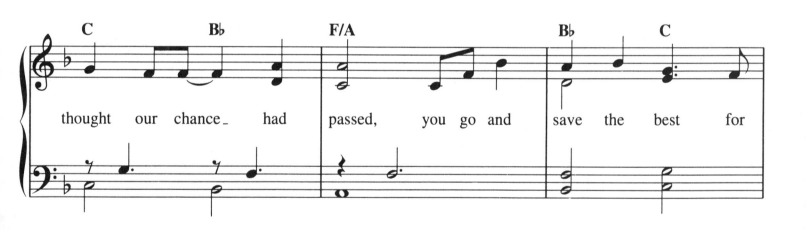

thought our chance_ had passed, you go and save the best for

1.
last.

All of the last.

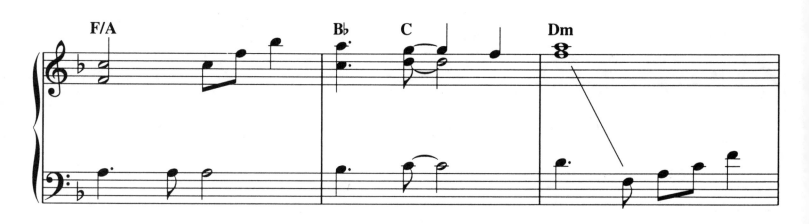

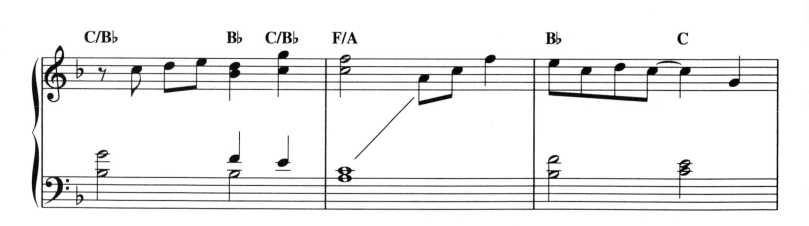

Some-times the ver - y thing _ you're look - ing for _ is the

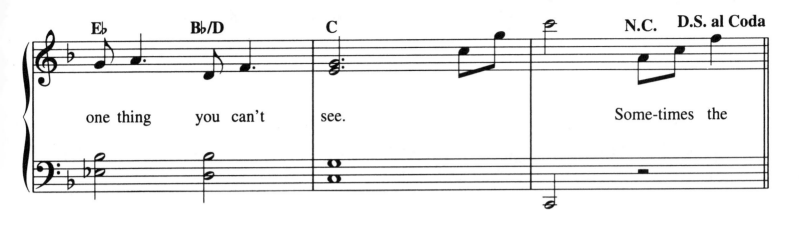

one thing you can't see. Some-times the

CODA

last.

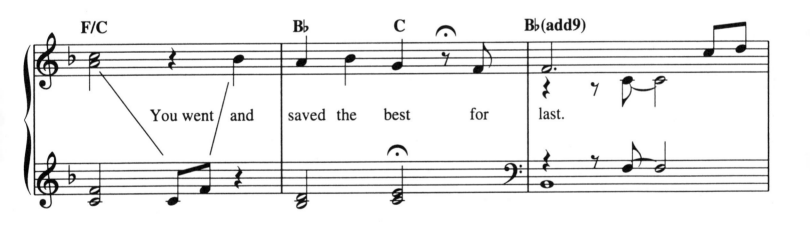

You went and saved the best for last.

LOVE OF A LIFETIME

Words and Music by BILL LEVERTY
and CARL SNARE

Slow Rock Ballad

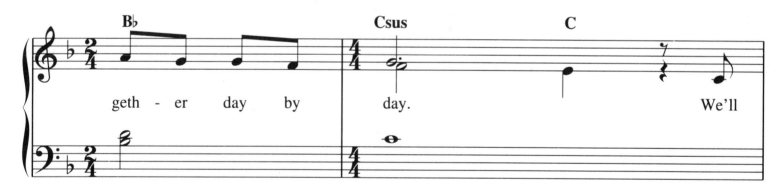

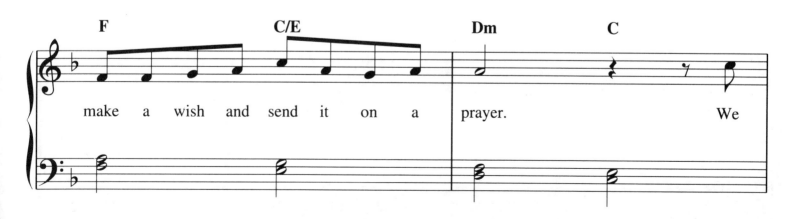

know our dreams can all come true with love that we can

share. With you I nev - er won - der,

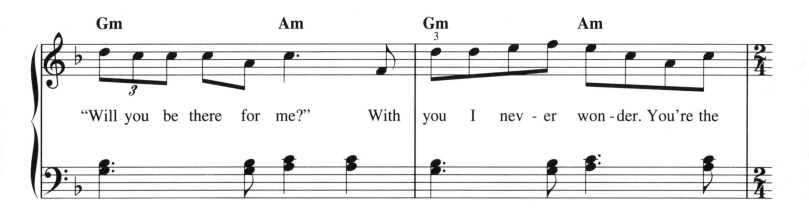

"Will you be there for me?" With you I nev - er won - der. You're the

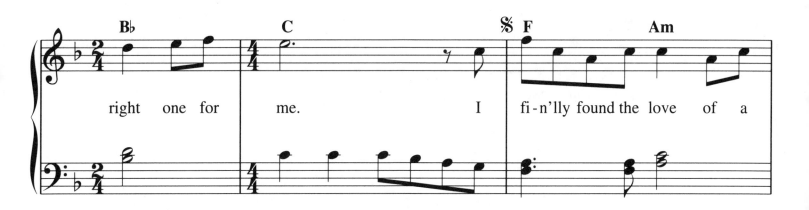

right one for me. I fi - n'lly found the love of a

life-time,   a love to last my whole life through.   I

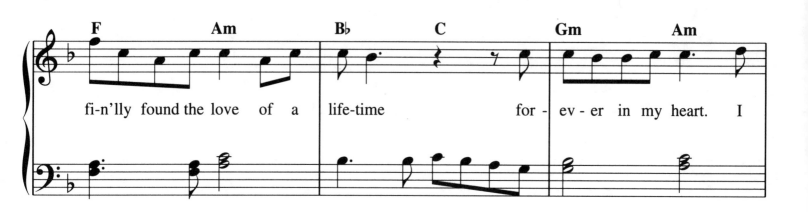

fi-n'lly found the love of a life-time   for - ev - er in my heart.   I

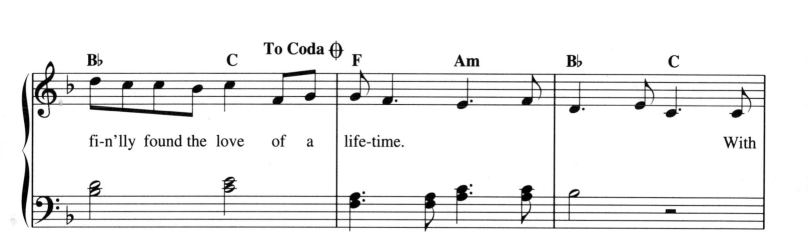

fi-n'lly found the love of a life-time.   With

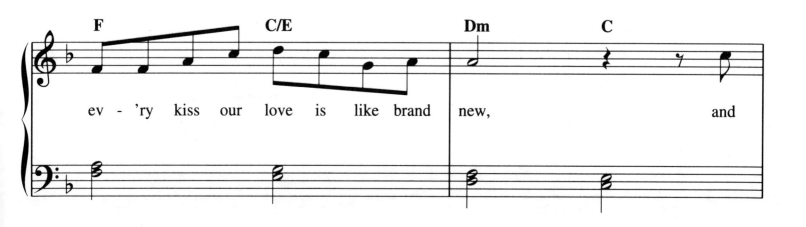

ev - 'ry kiss our love is like brand new,   and

ev - 'ry star up in the sky was made for me and you.

Still, we both know that the road is long, but we

know we'll be to - geth - er be - cause our love is strong. I

life-time.

LOVE OF MY LIFE

Words and Music by JIM BRICKMAN
and TOM DOUGLAS

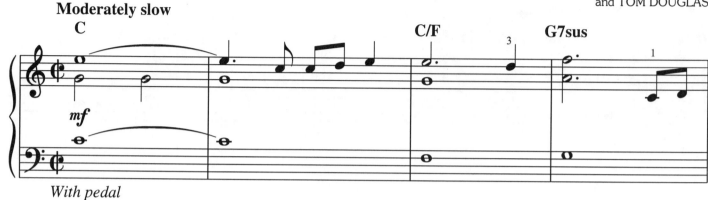

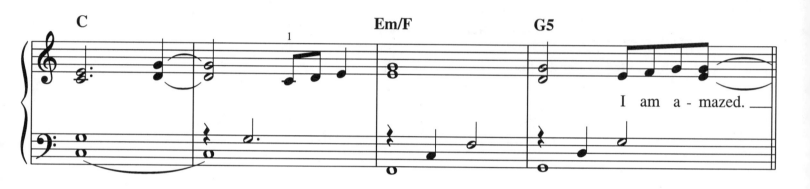

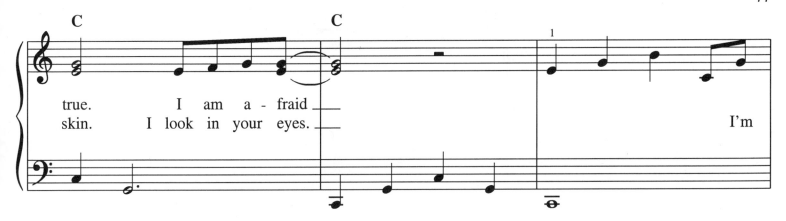

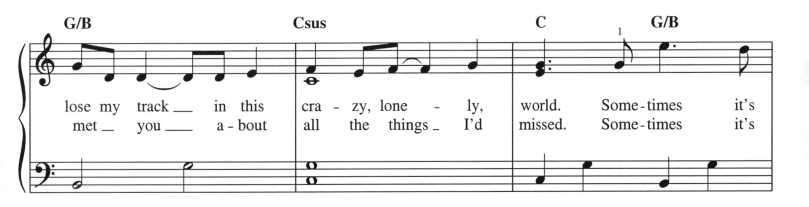

Now, here you | life.

You are the love

love, my an - gel in the night,

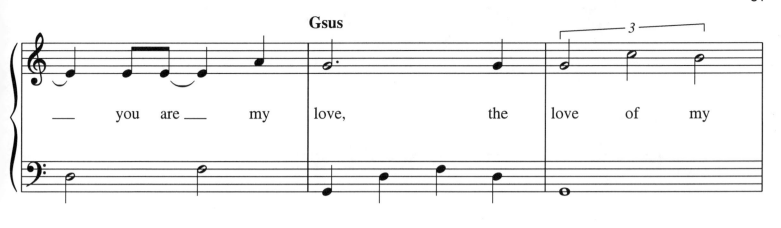

you are ___ my love, the love of my

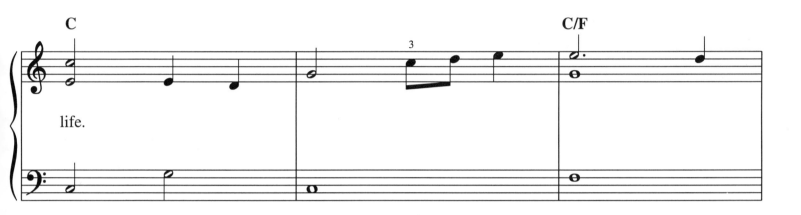

life.

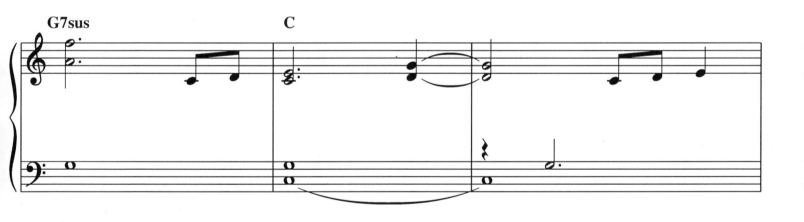

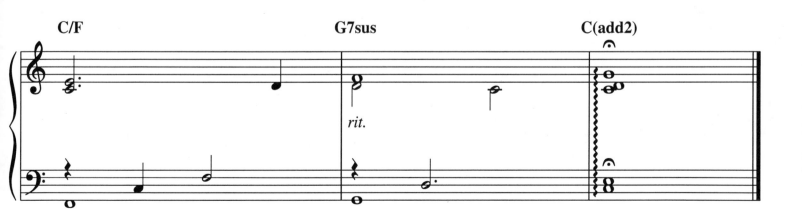

rit.

MY HEART WILL GO ON

(Love Theme from 'Titanic')

from the Paramount and Twentieth Century Fox Motion Picture TITANIC

Music by JAMES HORNER
Lyric by WILL JENNINGS

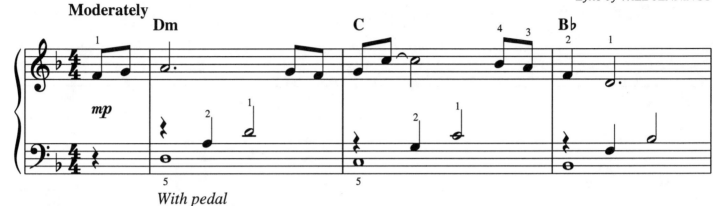

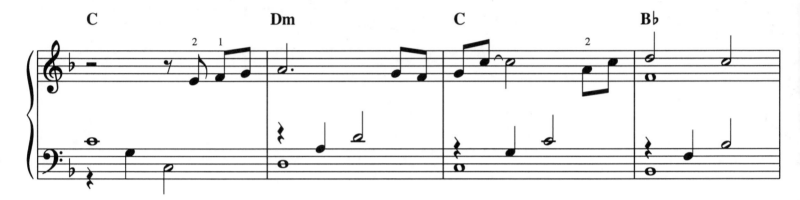

Ev - 'ry night in my dreams I see you, I

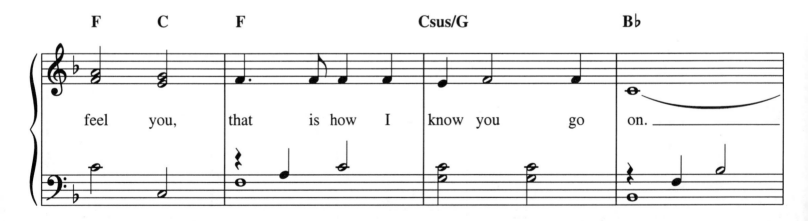

feel you, that is how I know you go on.

84

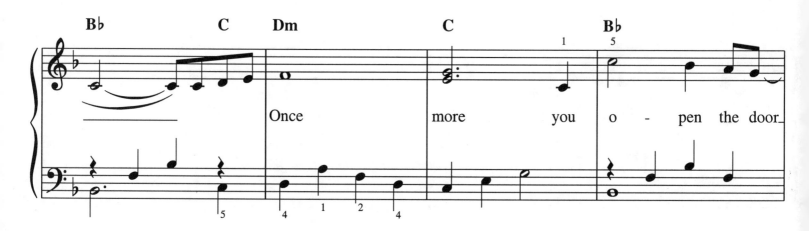

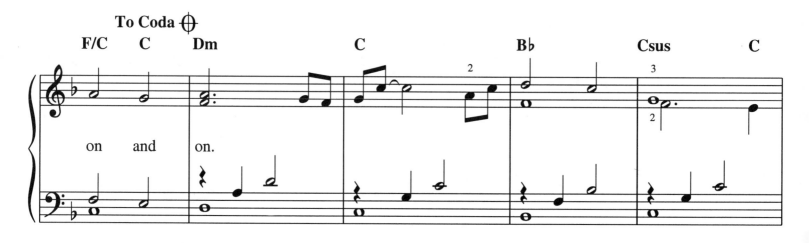

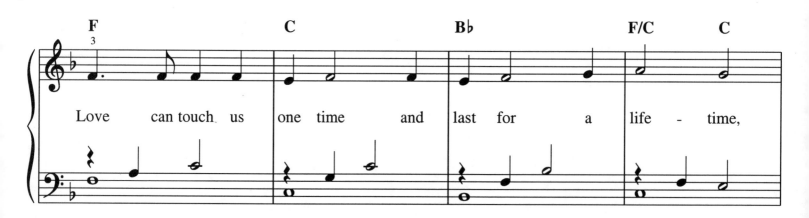

and nev-er let go till we're gone.

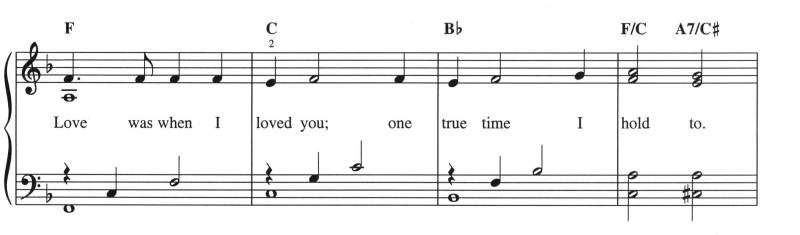

Love was when I loved you; one true time I hold to.

D.S. al Coda

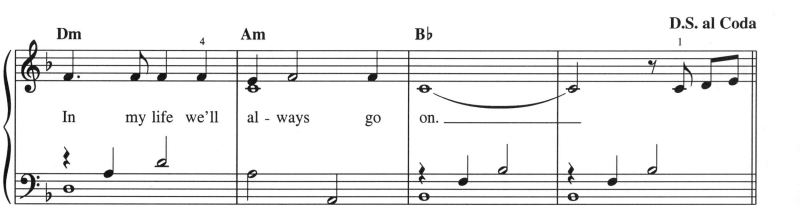

In my life we'll al-ways go on.

CODA

on.

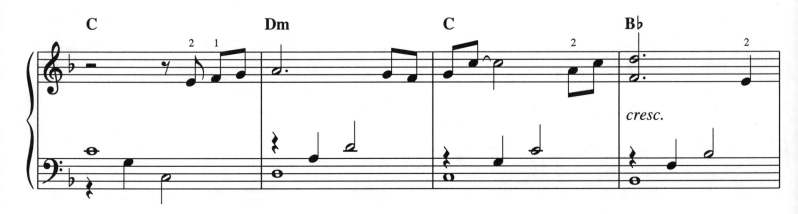

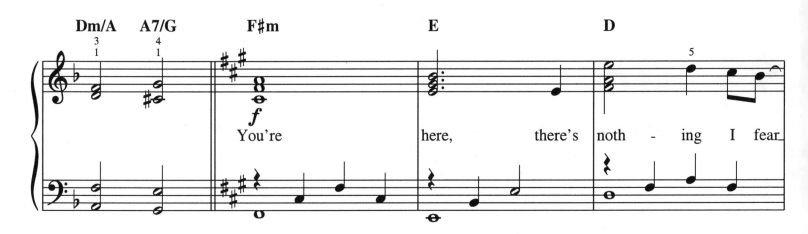

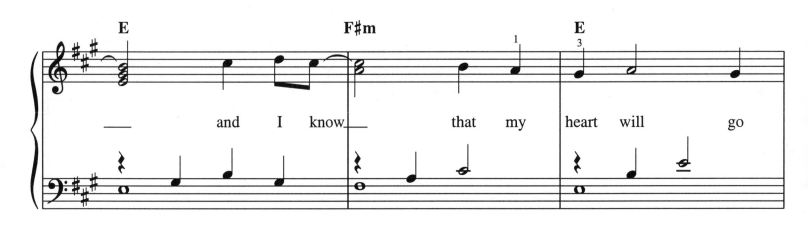

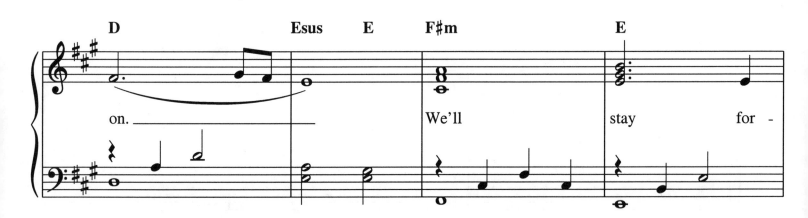

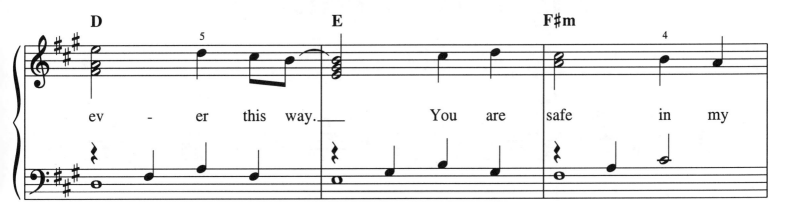

ev - er this way. You are safe in my

heart, and my heart will go on and on.
ff
decrescendo to end

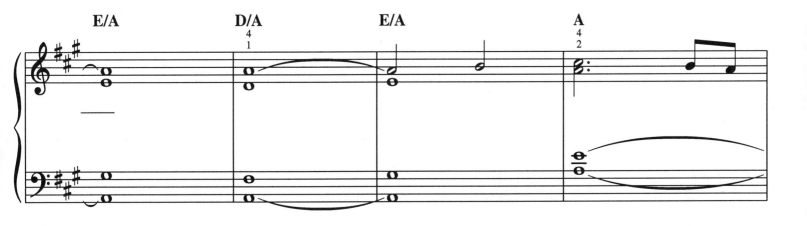

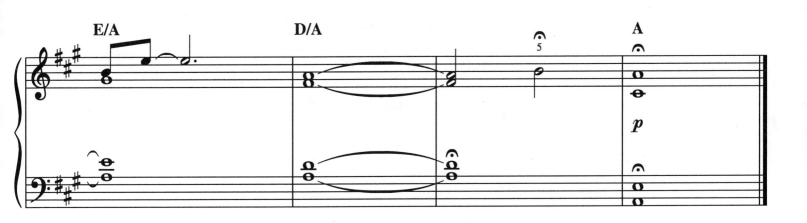

p

RIBBON IN THE SKY

Words and Music by
STEVIE WONDER

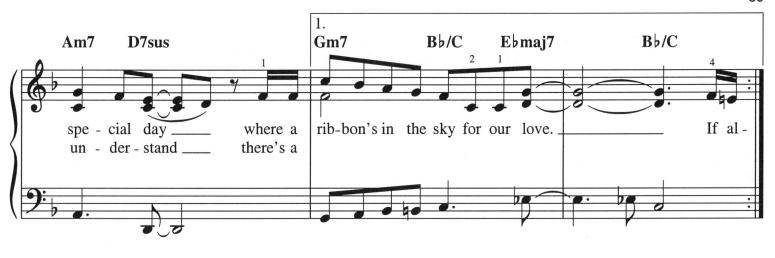

spe - cial day _____ where a rib-bon's in the sky for our love. _____ If al -
un - der - stand _____ there's a

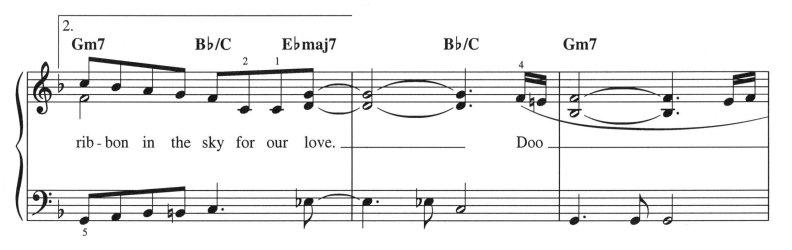

rib - bon in the sky for our love. _____ Doo

Doo doo _____

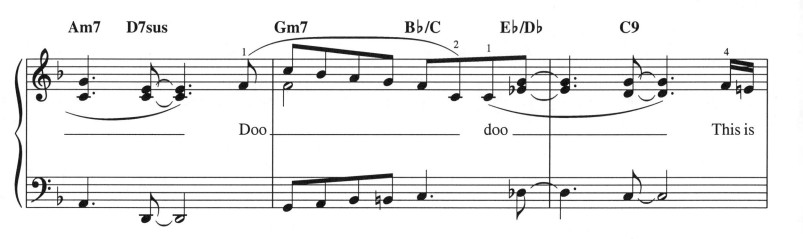

Doo _____ doo _____ This is

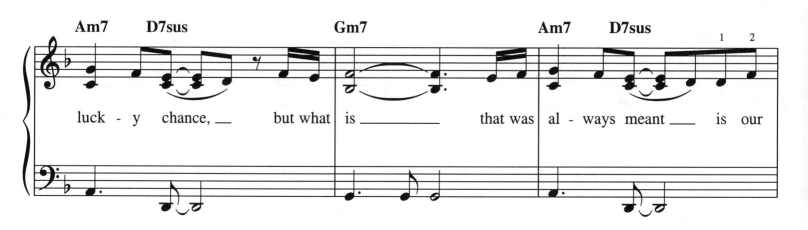

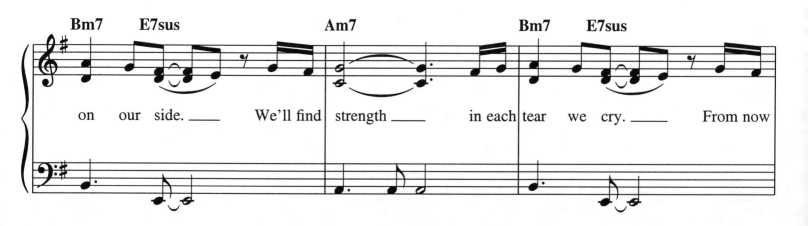

on _____ it will be you and I _____ and our rib-bon in the sky,

rib-bon in the sky, a rib-bon in the sky for our love. _____

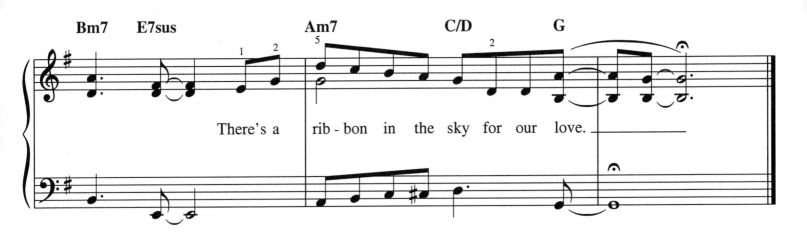

There's a rib-bon in the sky for our love. _____

SO AMAZING

Words and Music by
LUTHER VANDROSS

with pedal

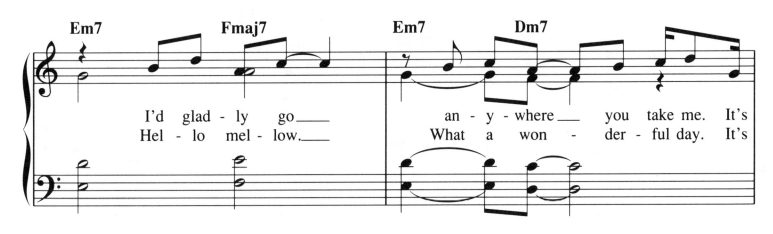

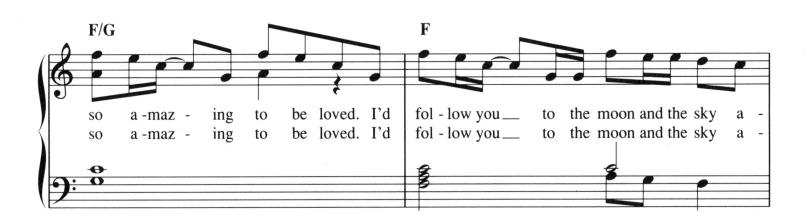

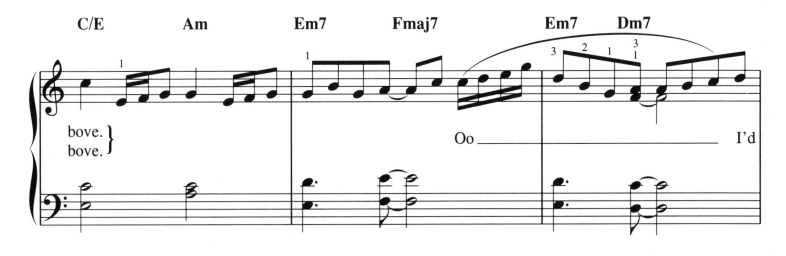

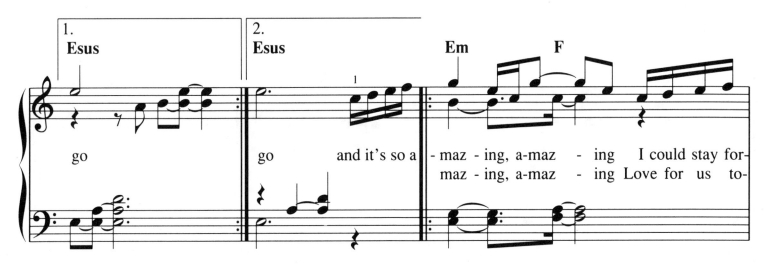

e - ver, for - ev - er. Here in love and won't leave you nev - er 'cause we've got a

geth - er, to - geth - er I would leave you nev - er and nev - er Guess we've got a

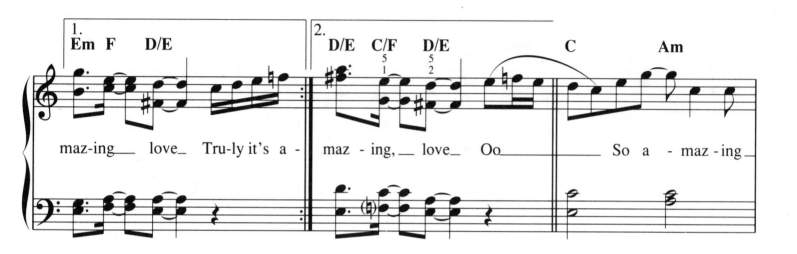

maz-ing__ love_ Tru-ly it's a - maz - ing,__ love_ Oo__ So a - maz - ing__

__ And I've been wait-ing,__ For a love like you, It's so a - maz - ing to be loved. I'd

fol-low you__ to the moon and the sky a - bove. It's

THROUGH THE YEARS

Words and Music by STEVE DORFF
and MARTY PANZER

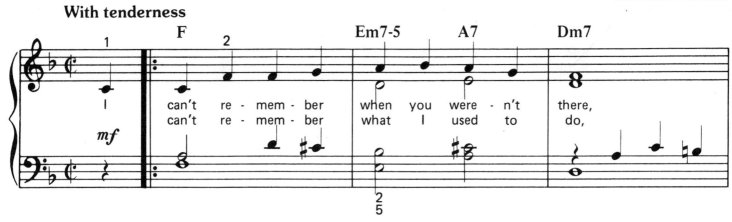

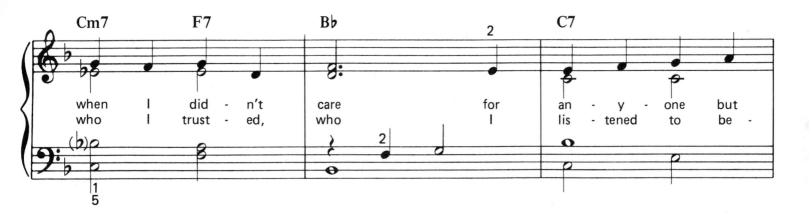

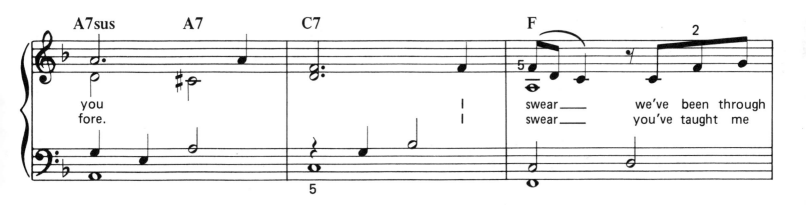

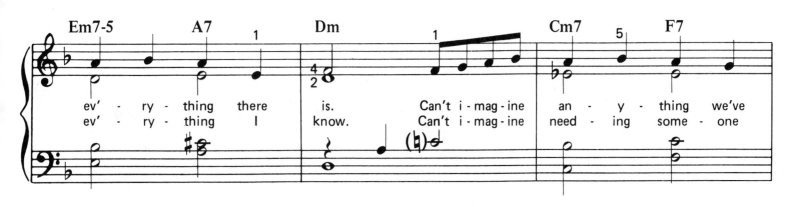

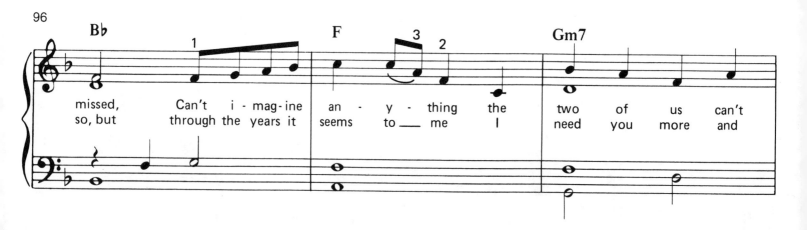

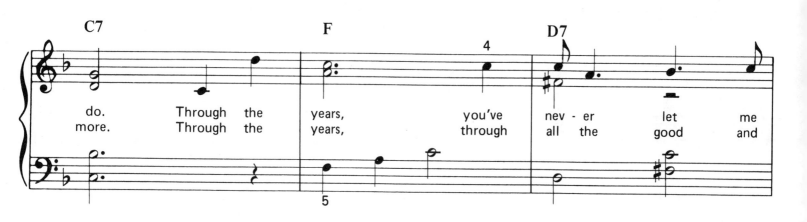

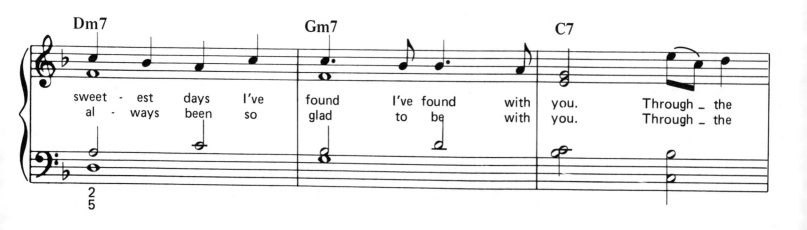

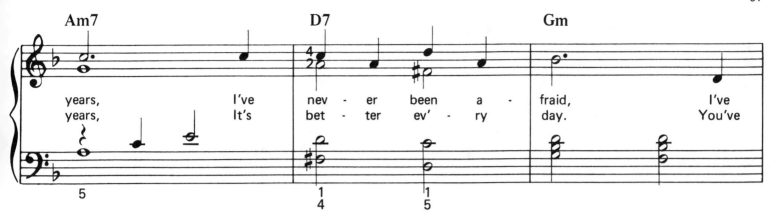

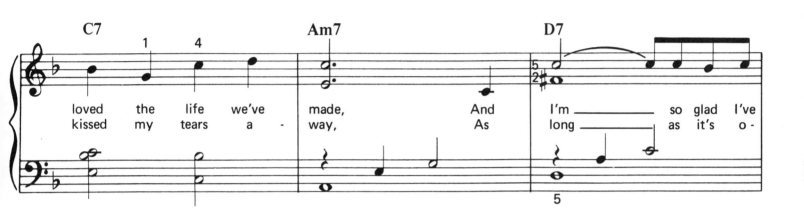

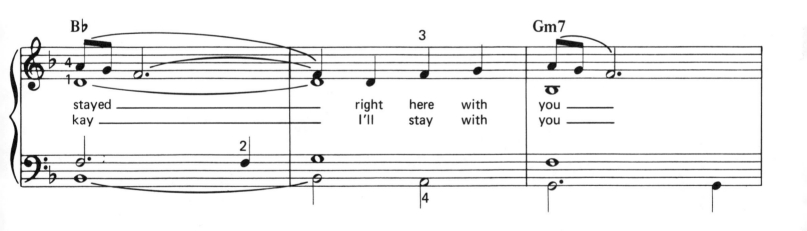

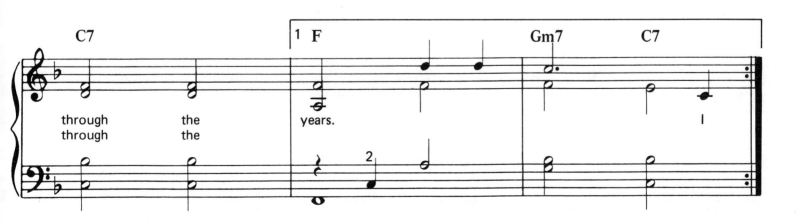

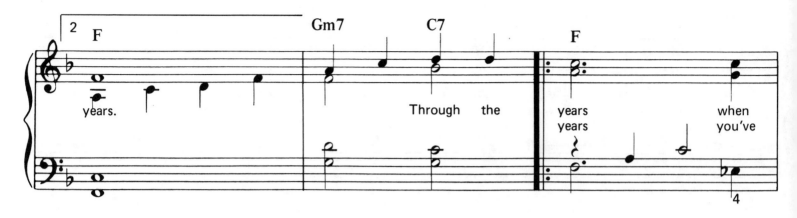

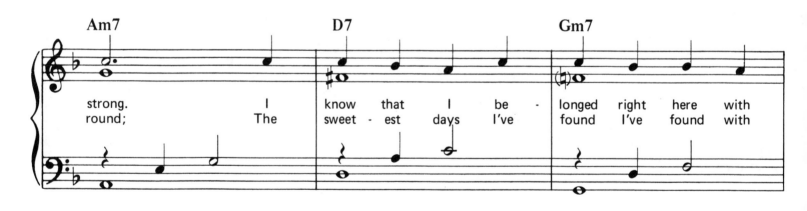

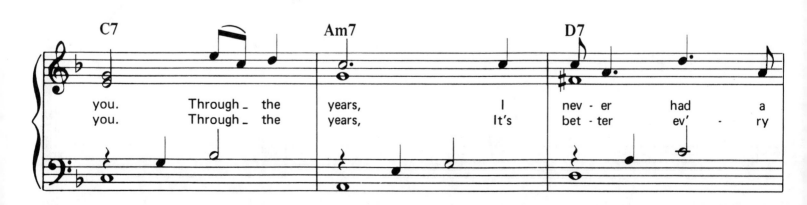

doubt   we'd   al - ways work things____ out   I've
day,   you've kissed my tears a - way   As

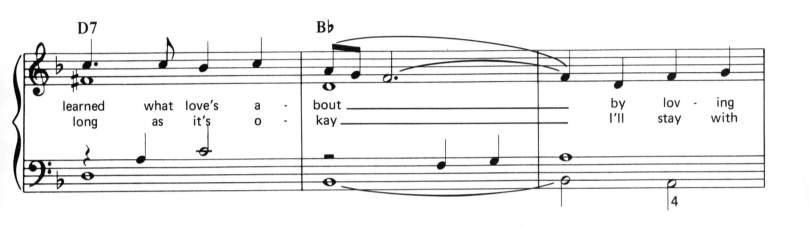

learned   what love's a - bout_____   by lov - ing
long   as it's o - kay_____   I'll stay with

you ____   through the years.   Through __ the
you ____   through the

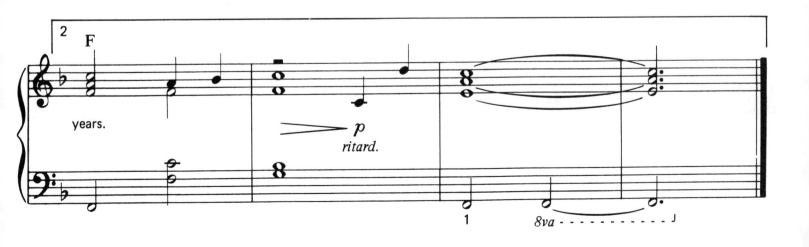

years.   *ritard.*

TEARS IN HEAVEN

featured in the Motion Picture RUSH

Words and Music by ERIC CLAPTON
and WILL JENNINGS

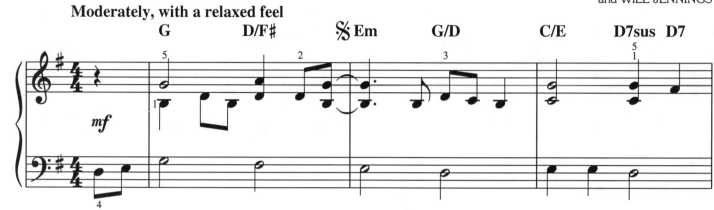

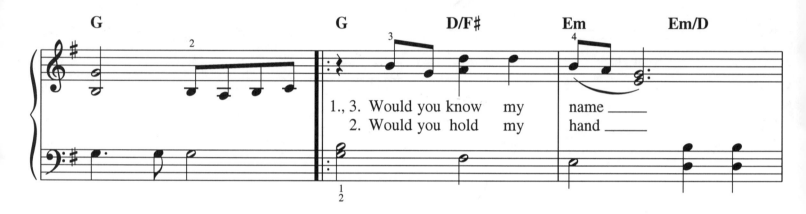

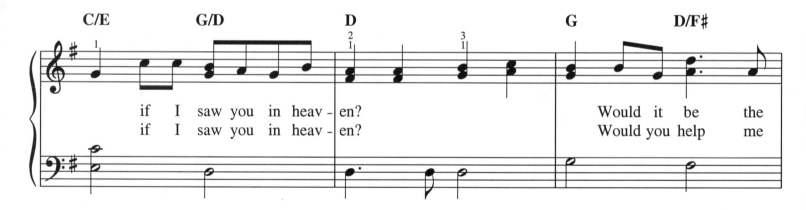

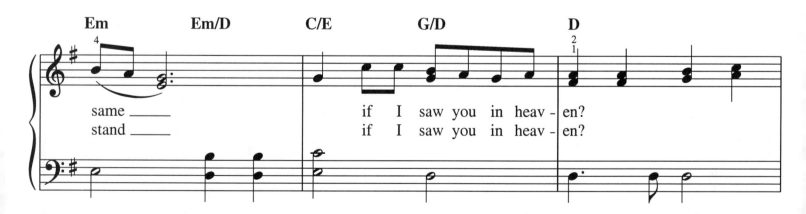

Time can bring you down, ___ time can bend your knees. ___

Time can break the heart, ___ have you beg - gin' please,

___ beg-gin' please. ___

(Instrumental)

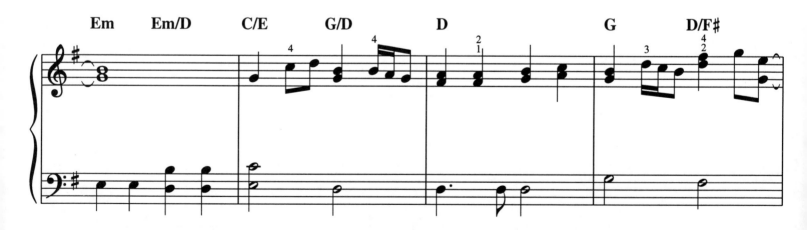

THANK GOD I FOUND YOU

Words and Music by MARIAH CAREY,
JAMES HARRIS III and TERRY LEWIS

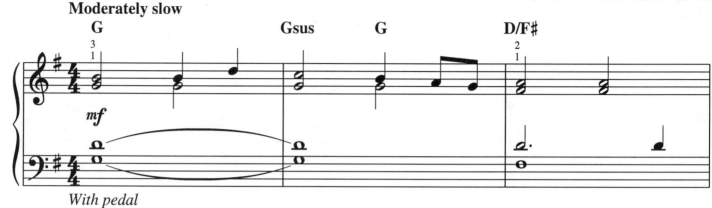

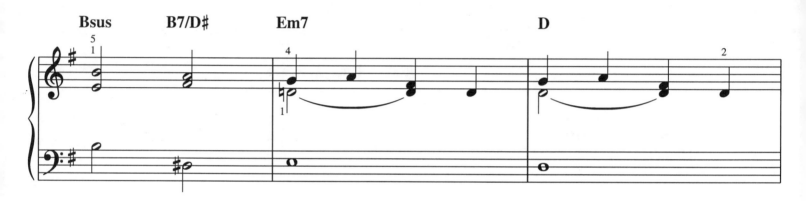

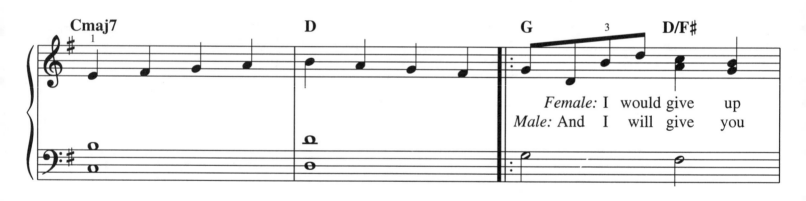

Female: I would give up
Male: And I will give you

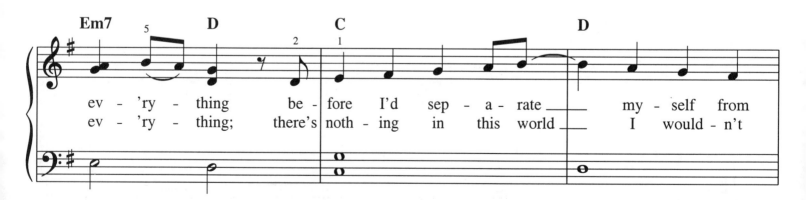

ev - 'ry - thing be - fore I'd sep - a - rate my - self from
ev - 'ry - thing; there's noth - ing in this world I would - n't

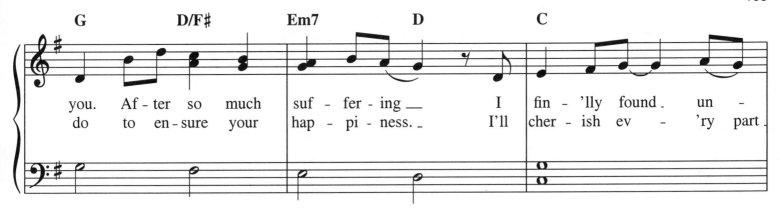

you. Af - ter so much suf - fer - ing ___ I fin - 'lly found ___ un -
do to en - sure your hap - pi - ness. ___ I'll cher - ish ev - 'ry part ___

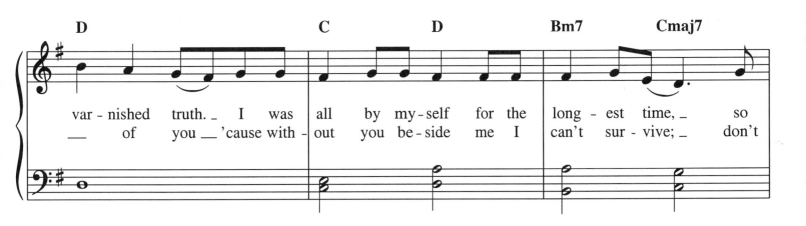

var - nished truth. ___ I was all by my - self for the long - est time, ___ so
___ of you ___ 'cause with - out you be - side me I can't sur - vive; ___ don't

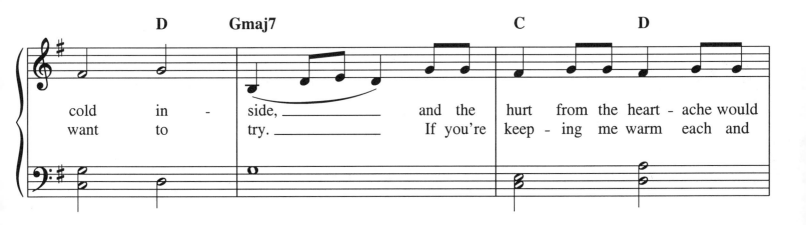

cold in - side, _____ and the hurt from the heart - ache would
want to try. _____ If you're keep - ing me warm each and

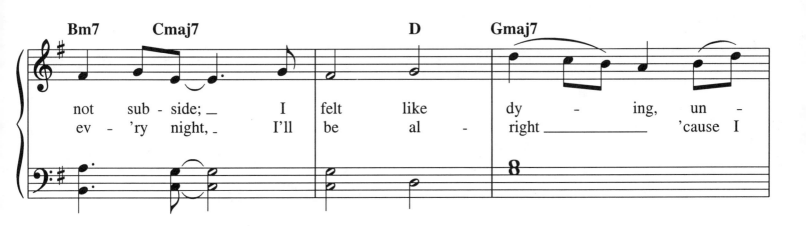

not sub - side; ___ I felt like dy - ing, un -
ev - 'ry night, ___ I'll be al - right _____ 'cause I

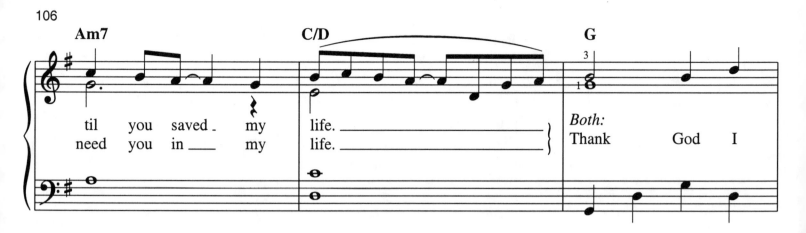

til you saved __ my life. _____
need you in ___ my life. _____ } *Both:* Thank God I

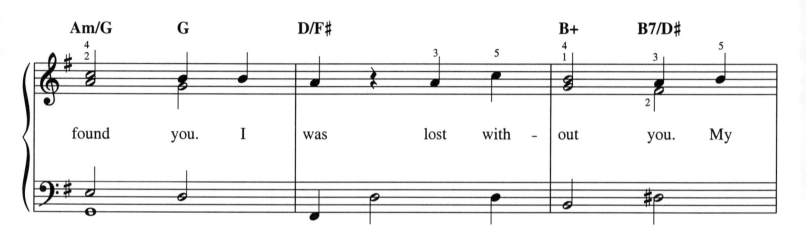

found you. I was lost with – out you. My

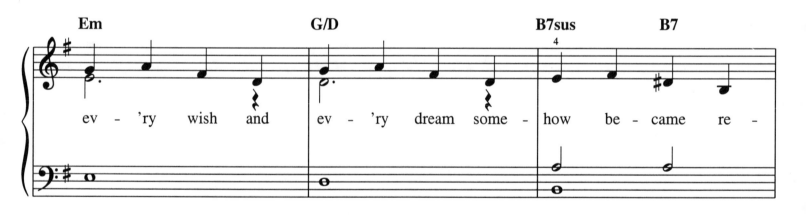

ev – 'ry wish and ev – 'ry dream some – how be – came re –

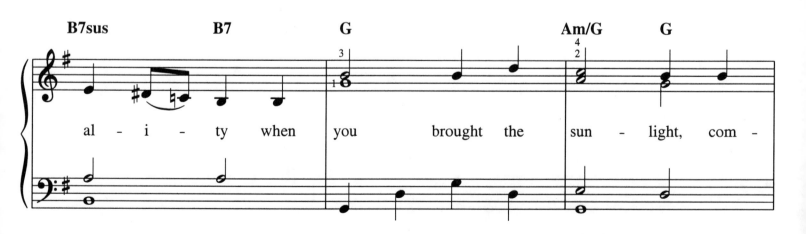

al – i – ty when you brought the sun – light, com –

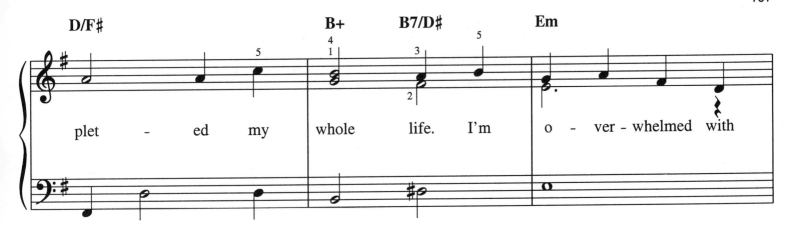

D/F♯ ... **B+** ... **B7/D♯** ... **Em**

plet - ed my whole life. I'm o - ver - whelmed with

G/D ... **Cmaj7** ... **D**

grat - i - tude 'cause ba - by, I'm so thank - ful I found

1. **G** ... **D/F♯** ... **Em** ... **D/F♯** ... **Cmaj7**

you. _____

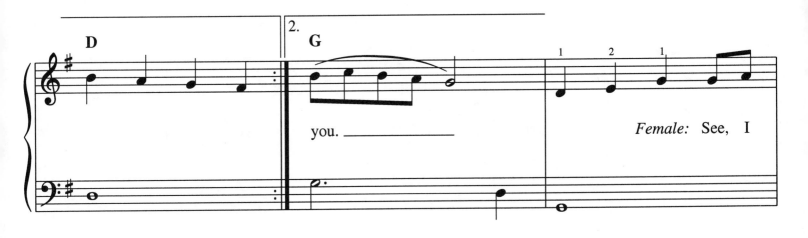

D ... 2. **G**

you. _____ *Female:* See, I

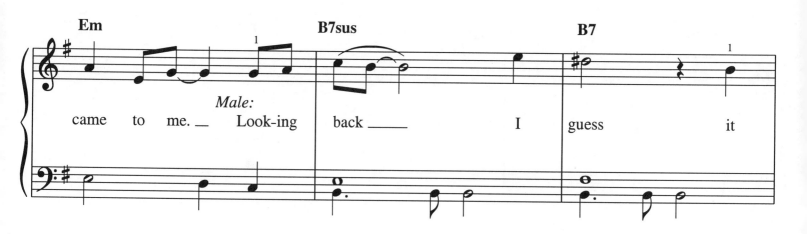

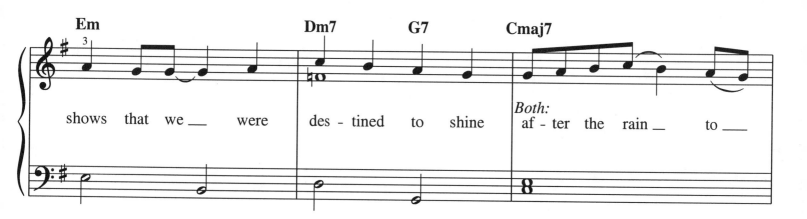

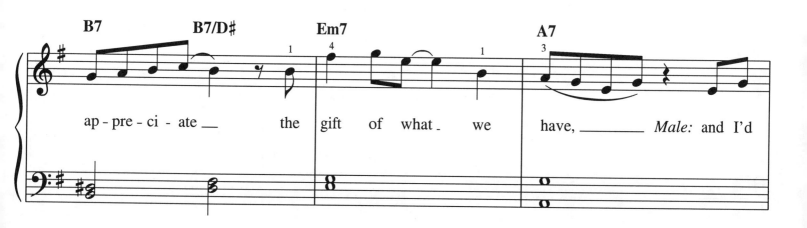

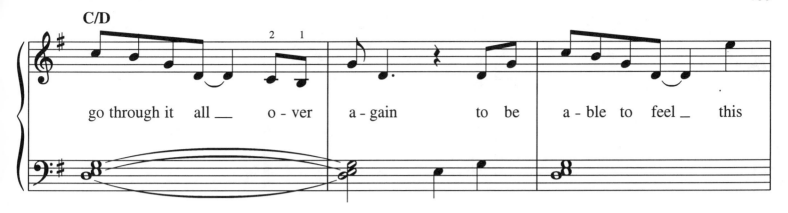

go through it all _ o - ver a - gain to be a - ble to feel _ this

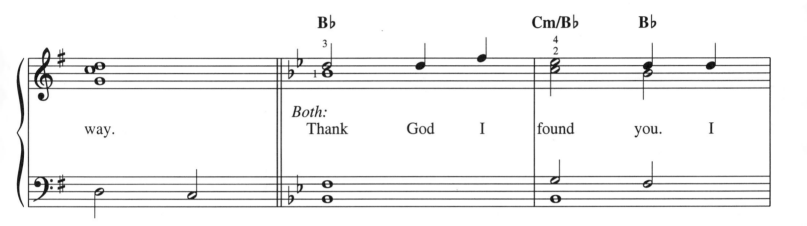

way. *Both:* Thank God I found you. I

was lost with - out you. My ev – 'ry wish and

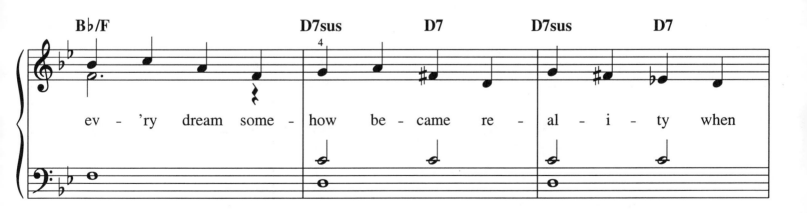

ev – 'ry dream some - how be - came re - al – i - ty when

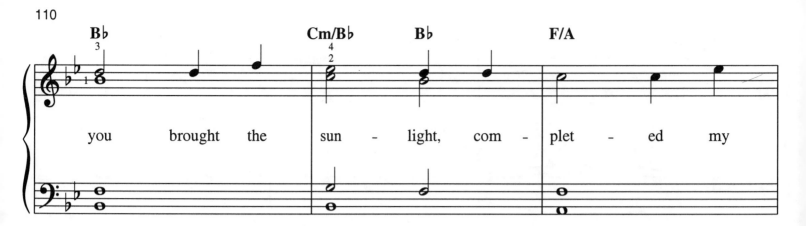

you brought the sun - light, com - plet - ed my

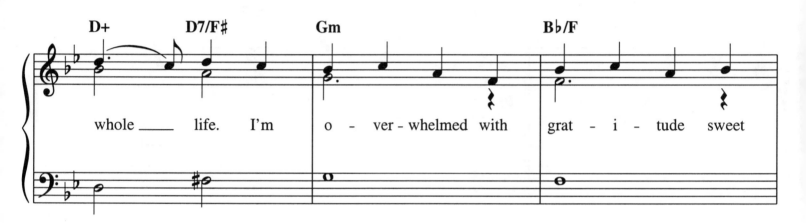

whole ___ life. I'm o - ver - whelmed with grat - i - tude sweet

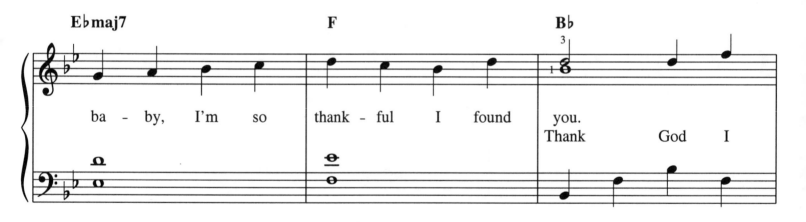

ba - by, I'm so thank - ful I found you.
Thank God I

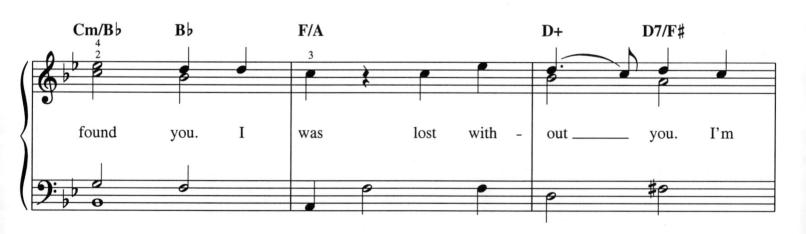

found you. I was lost with - out ___ you. I'm

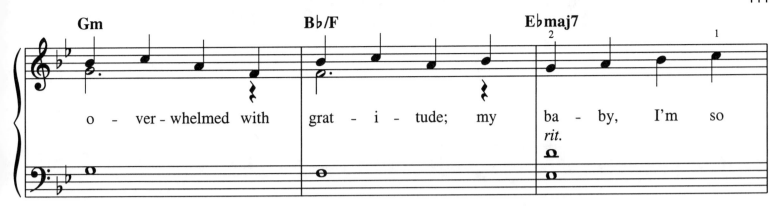

o - ver - whelmed with grat - i - tude; my ba — by, I'm so

thank - ful I found __ you.

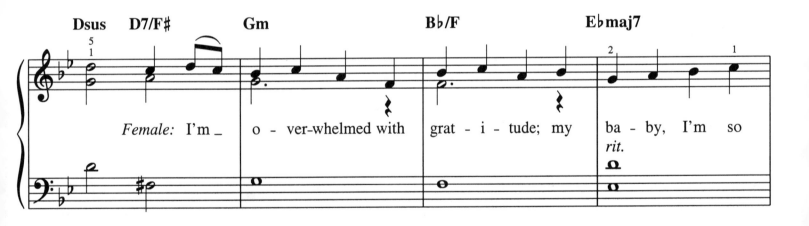

Female: I'm __ o - ver - whelmed with grat - i - tude; my ba - by, I'm so

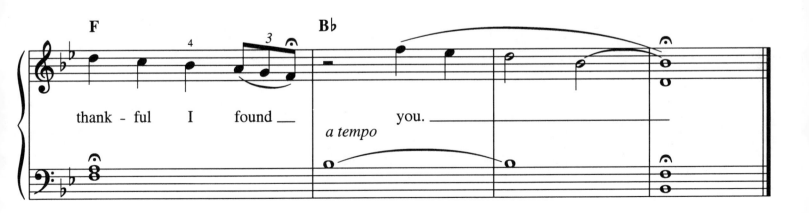

thank - ful I found __ you. __

TO LOVE YOU MORE

Words and Music by DAVID FOSTER
and JUNIOR MILES

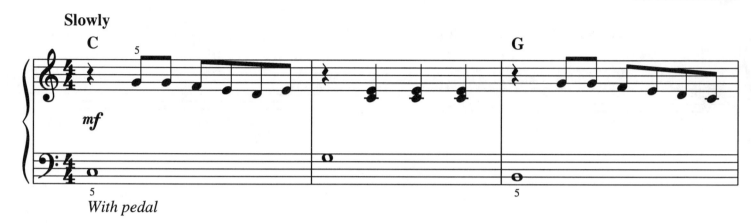

Take   me

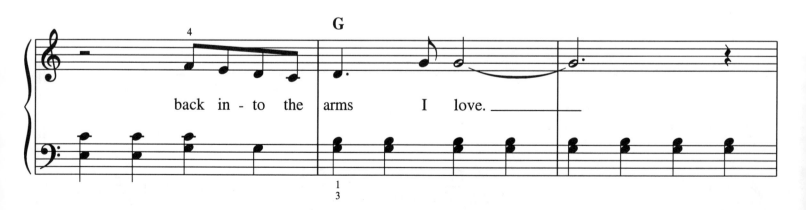

back in - to the   arms   I   love. _____

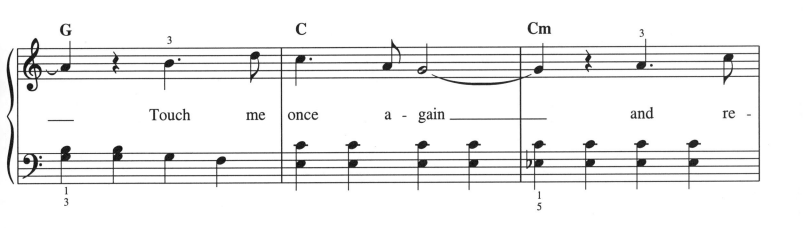

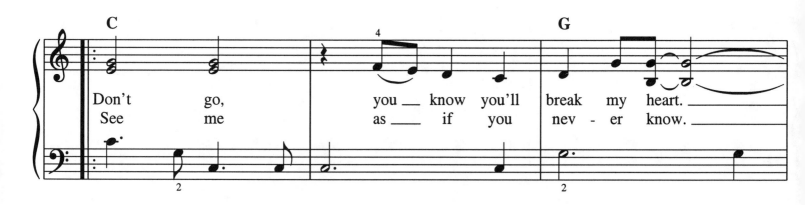

Don't go, you __ know you'll break my heart. __
See me as __ if you nev - er know. __

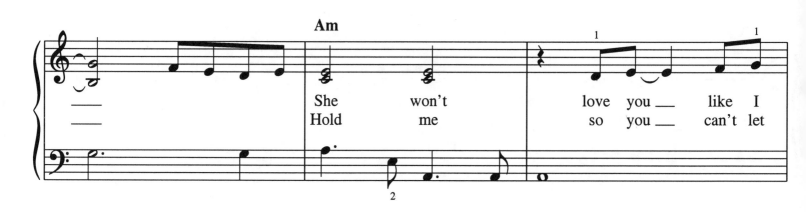

__ She won't love you __ like I
__ Hold me so you __ can't let

will. I'm the one who'll stay
go. Just be - lieve in me.

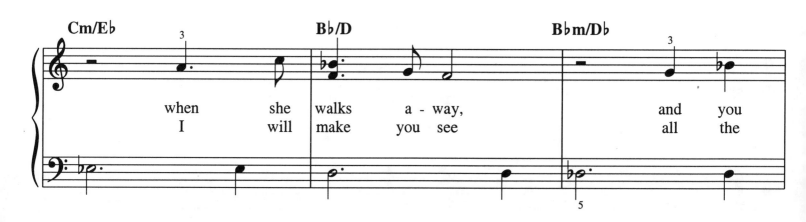

when she walks a - way, and you
I will make you see all the

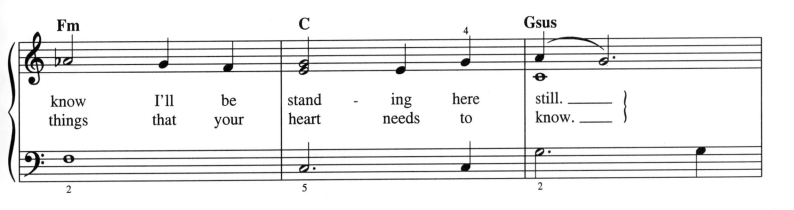

know I'll be stand - ing here still. _____
things that your heart needs to know. _____

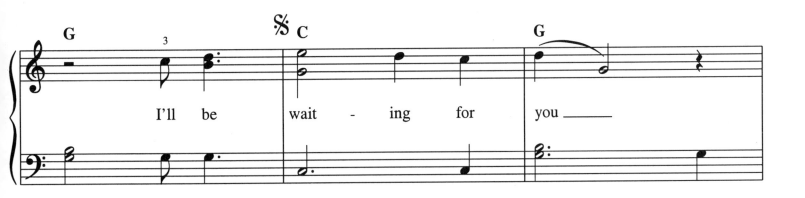

I'll be wait - ing for you _____

here in - side _____ my heart. I'm the one who wants _ to

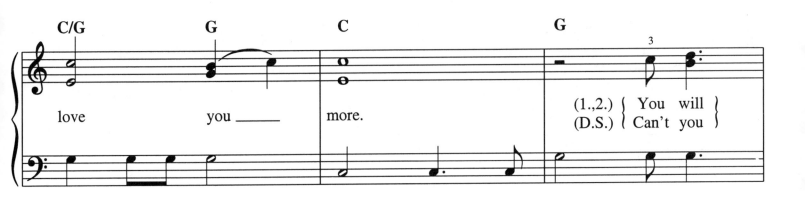

love you _____ more. (1., 2.) { You will }
(D.S.) { Can't you }

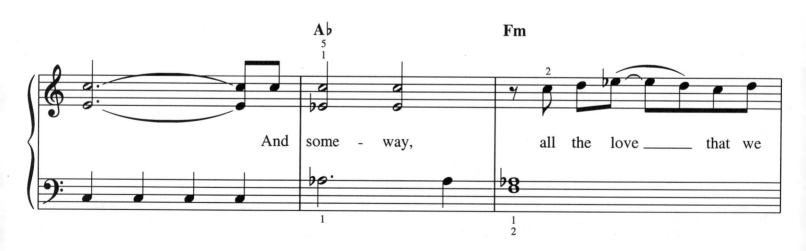

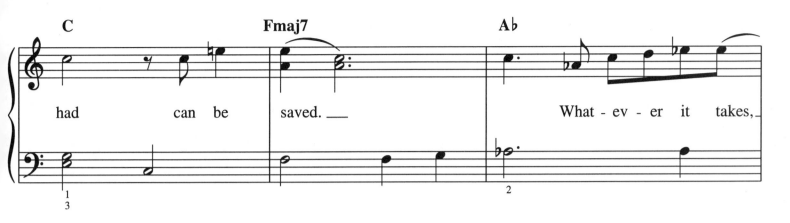

had   can be   saved. ___   What - ev - er it takes,

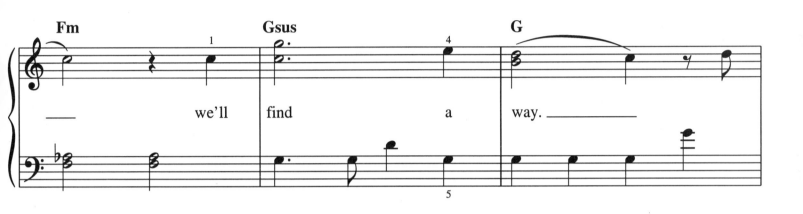

___   we'll   find   a   way. ___

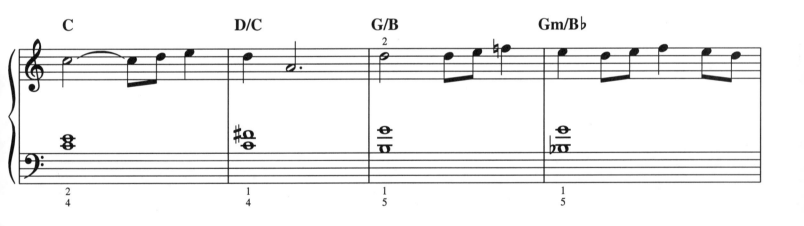

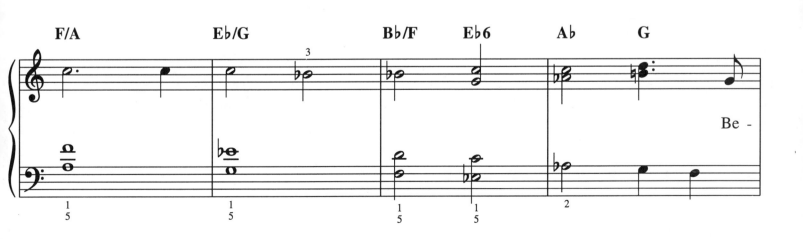

Be -

lieve in me.   I will make you see   all the

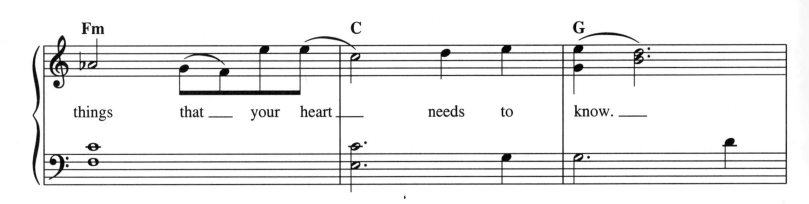

things   that ___ your heart ___   needs to   know. ___

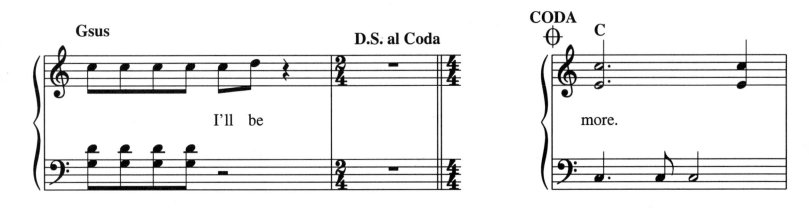

I'll be   more.

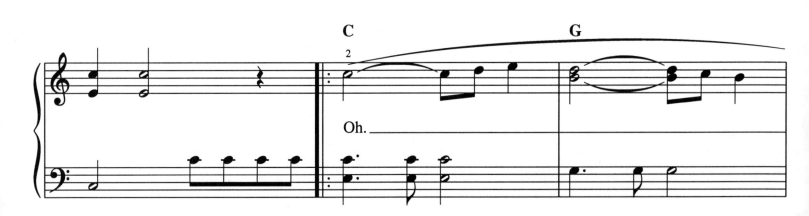

Oh. ___

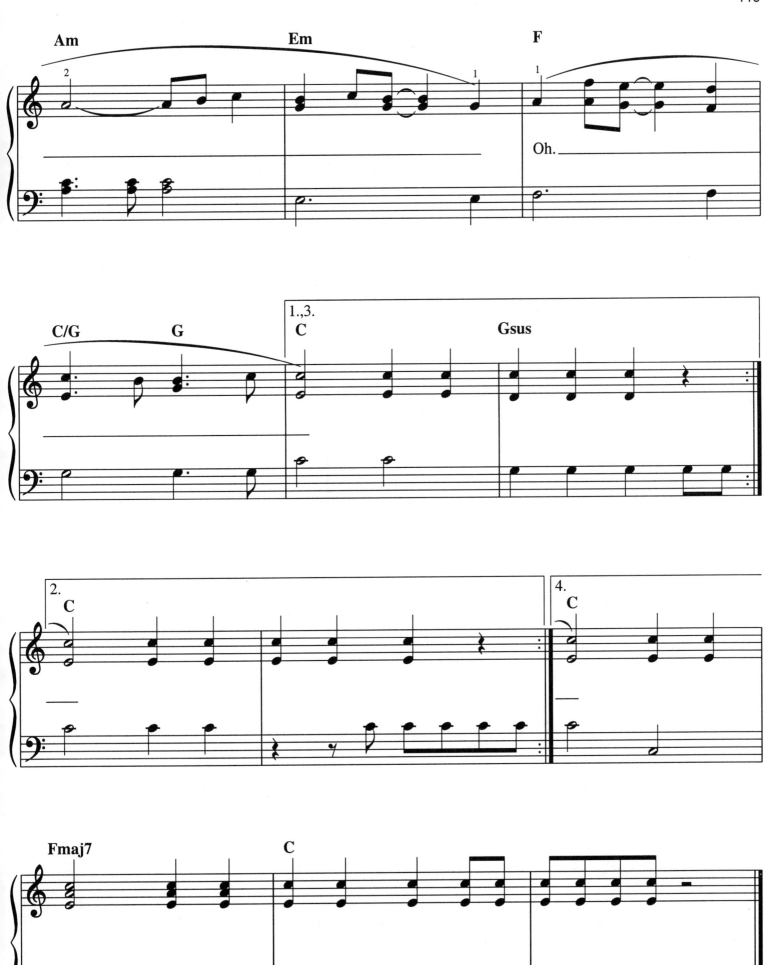

VALENTINE

Words and Music by JACK KUGELL
and JIM BRICKMAN

Moderately, with expression

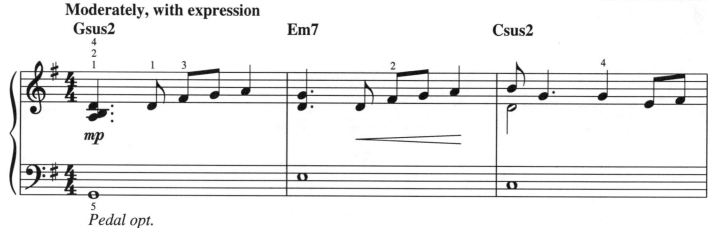

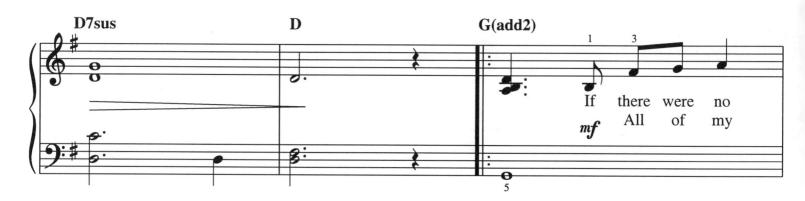

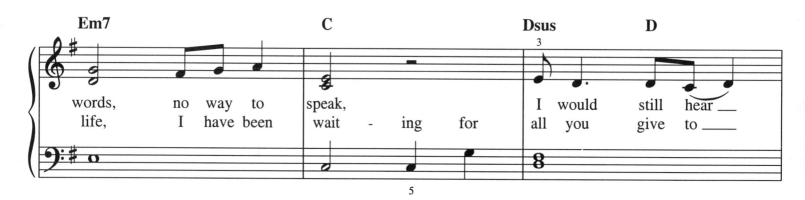

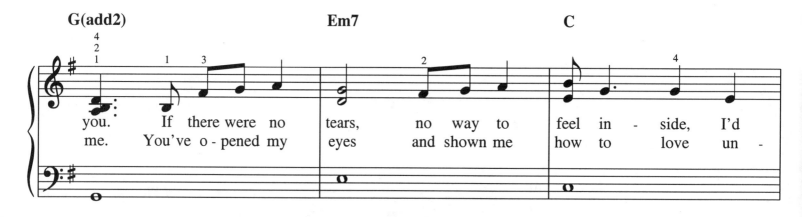

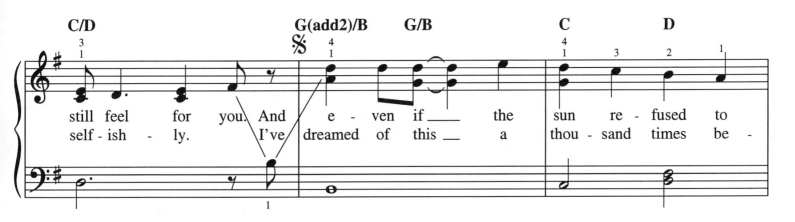

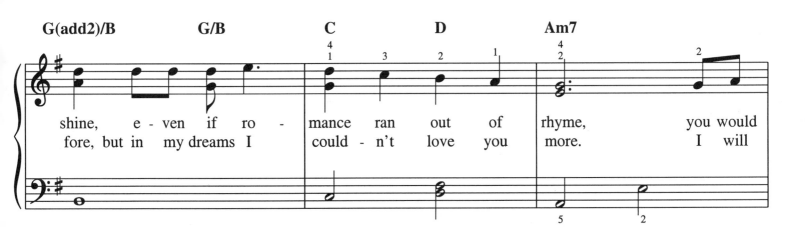

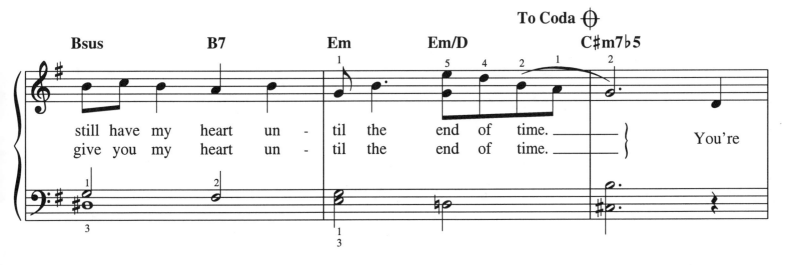

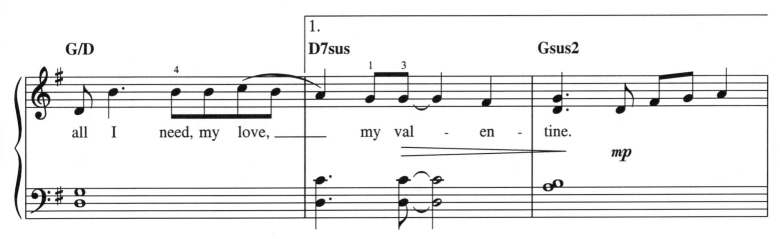

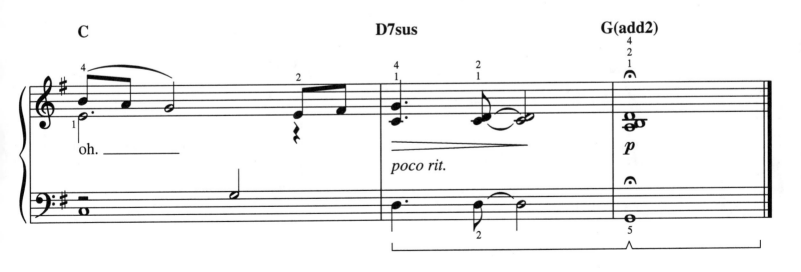

VISION OF LOVE

Words and Music by MARIAH CAREY
and BEN MARGULIES

lieved _____
lieved _____
    some-how the   one that I need - ed
    and now I   know I've suc - ceed - ed

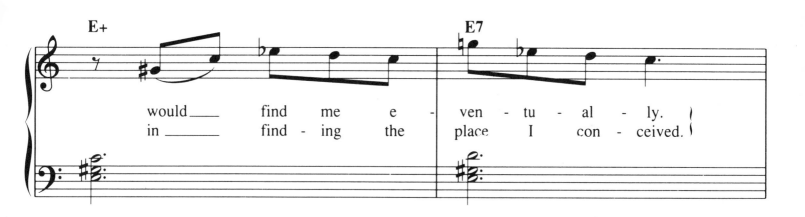

would ___ find me e - ven - tu - al - ly.
in ___ find - ing the place I con - ceived.

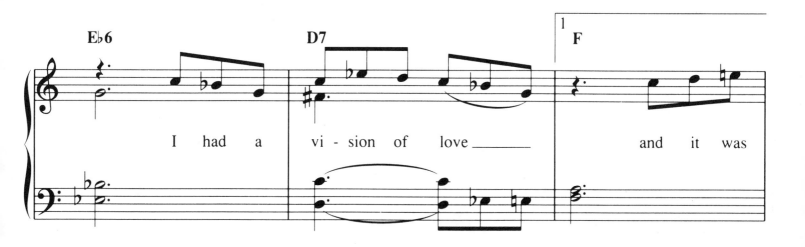

I had a   vi - sion of love _____   and it was

all that you've giv - en to me. _____

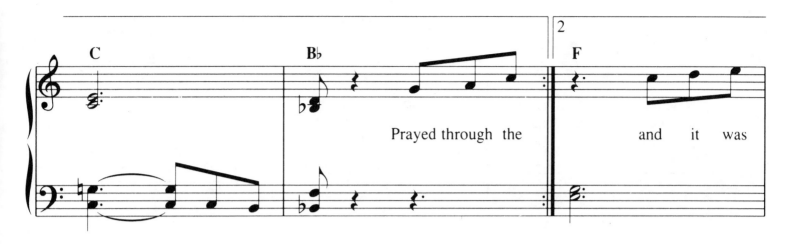

Prayed through the

and it was

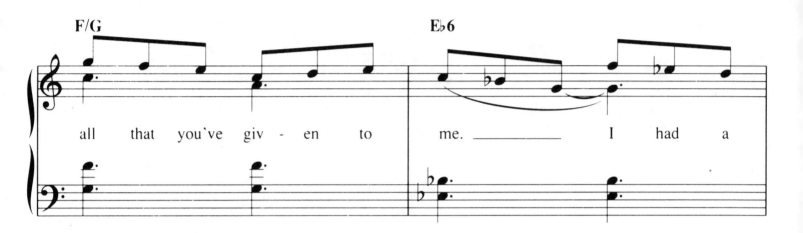

all that you've giv - en to me. _____ I had a

vi - sion of love _____ and it was all that you've giv - en me.

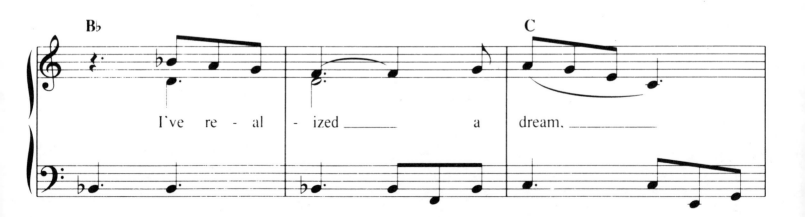

I've re - al - ized _____ a dream. _____

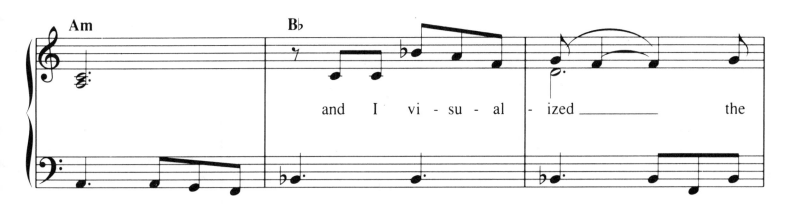

and I vi - su - al - ized _____ the

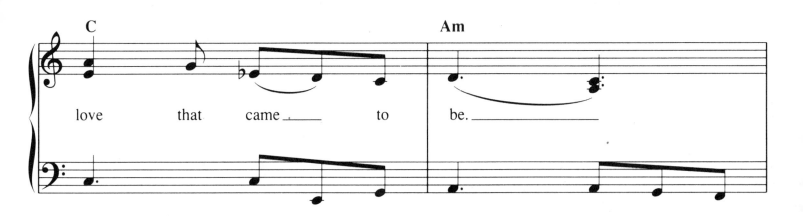

love that came ___ to be. _____

Feel ___ so a - live. _____ I'm so thank - ful that I've re -

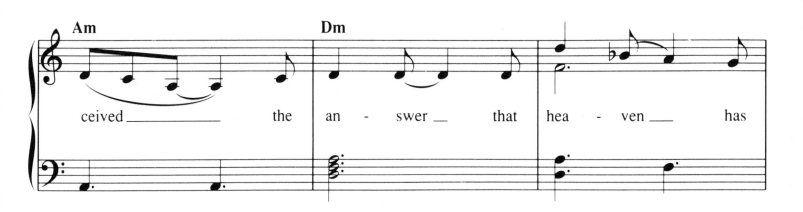

ceived _____ the an - swer ___ that hea - ven ___ has

sent down to me. You treat - ed me kind, _____

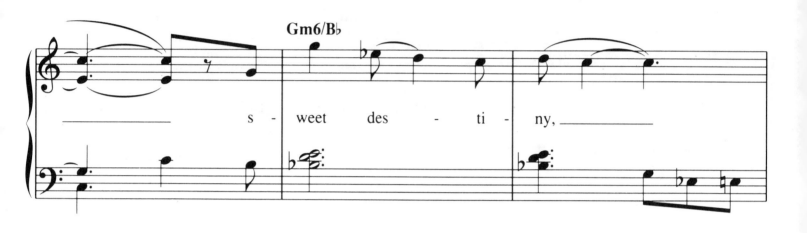

_____ s - weet des - ti - ny, _____

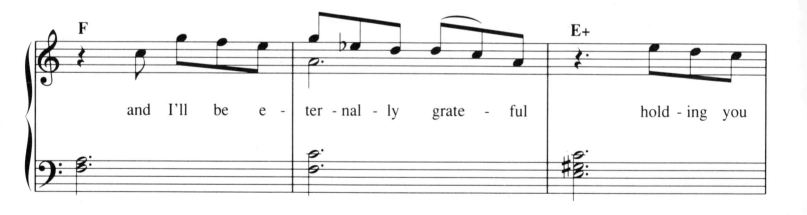

and I'll be e - ter - nal - ly grate - ful hold - ing you

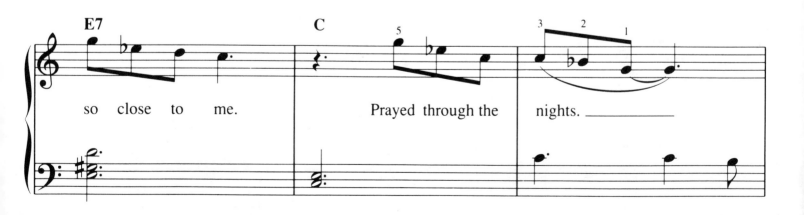

so close to me. Prayed through the nights. _____

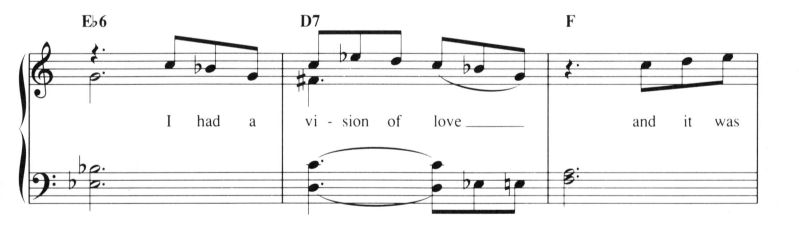

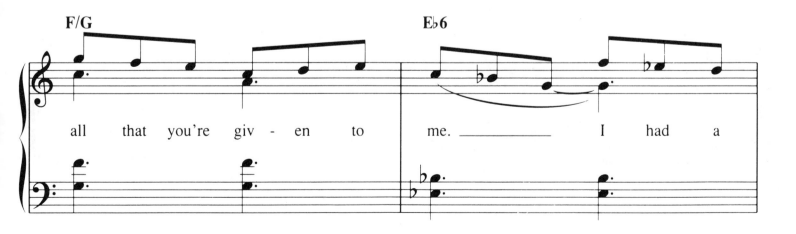

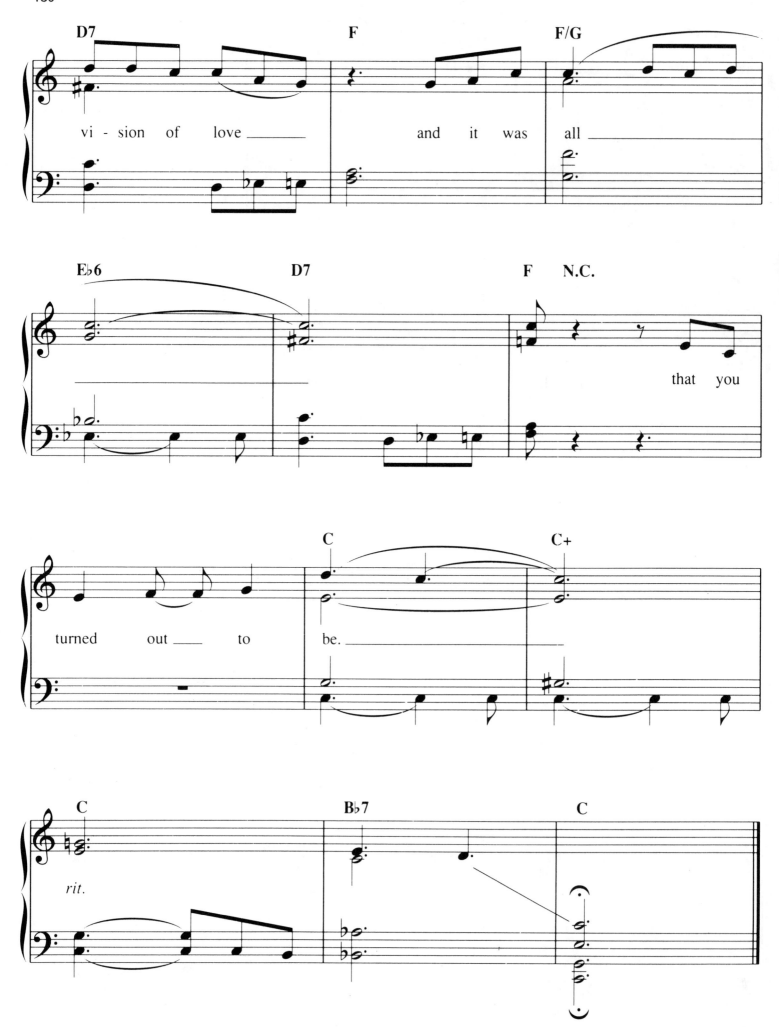

A WHOLE NEW WORLD
(Aladdin's Theme)
from Walt Disney's ALADDIN

Music by ALAN MENKEN
Lyrics by TIM RICE

Slowly and sweetly

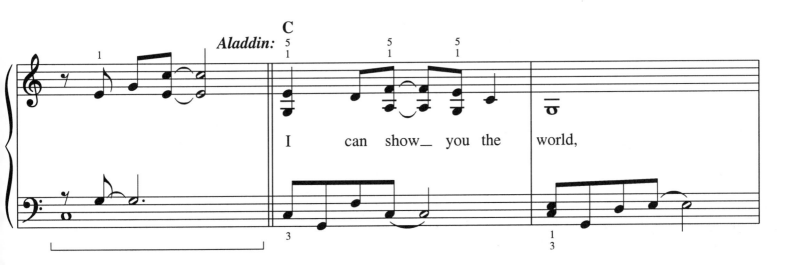

I can show__ you the world,

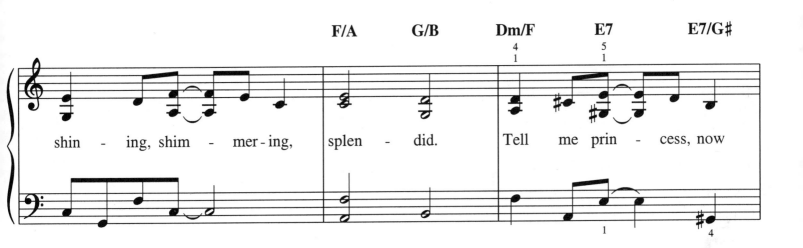

shin - ing, shim - mer - ing, splen - did. Tell me prin - cess, now

when did you last let your heart _ de - cide?

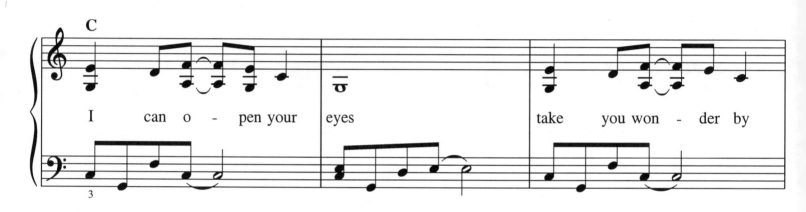

I can o - pen your eyes take you won - der by

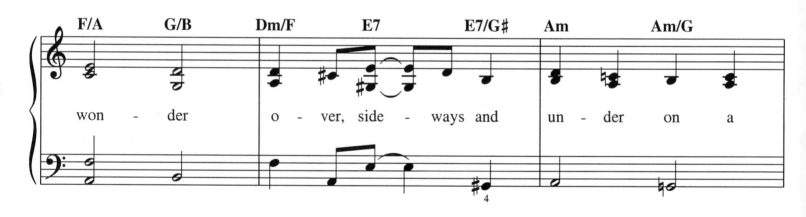

won - der o - ver, side - ways and un - der on a

mag - ic car - pet ride. A whole new world

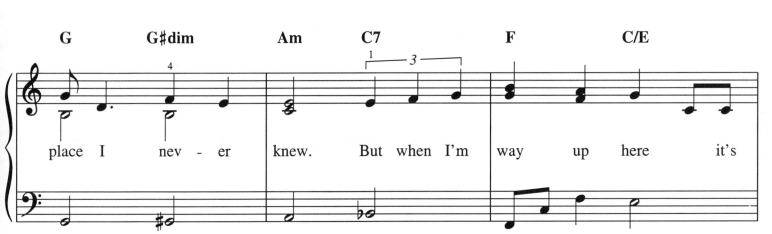

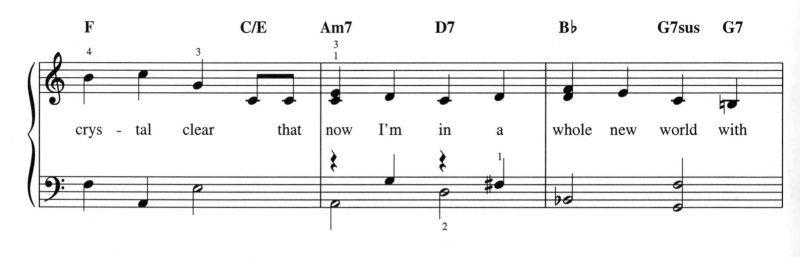

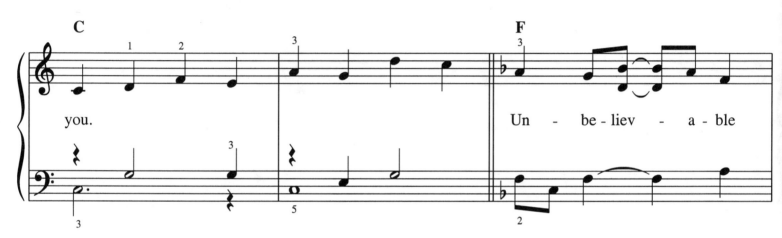

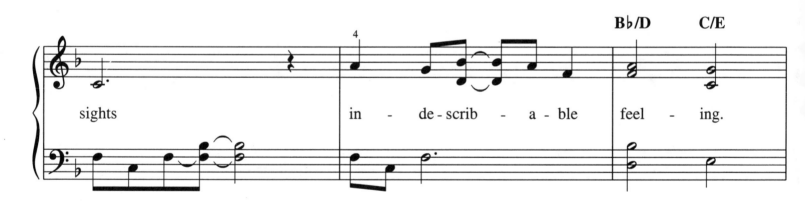

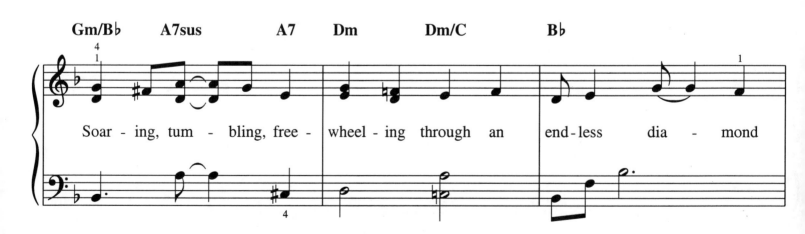

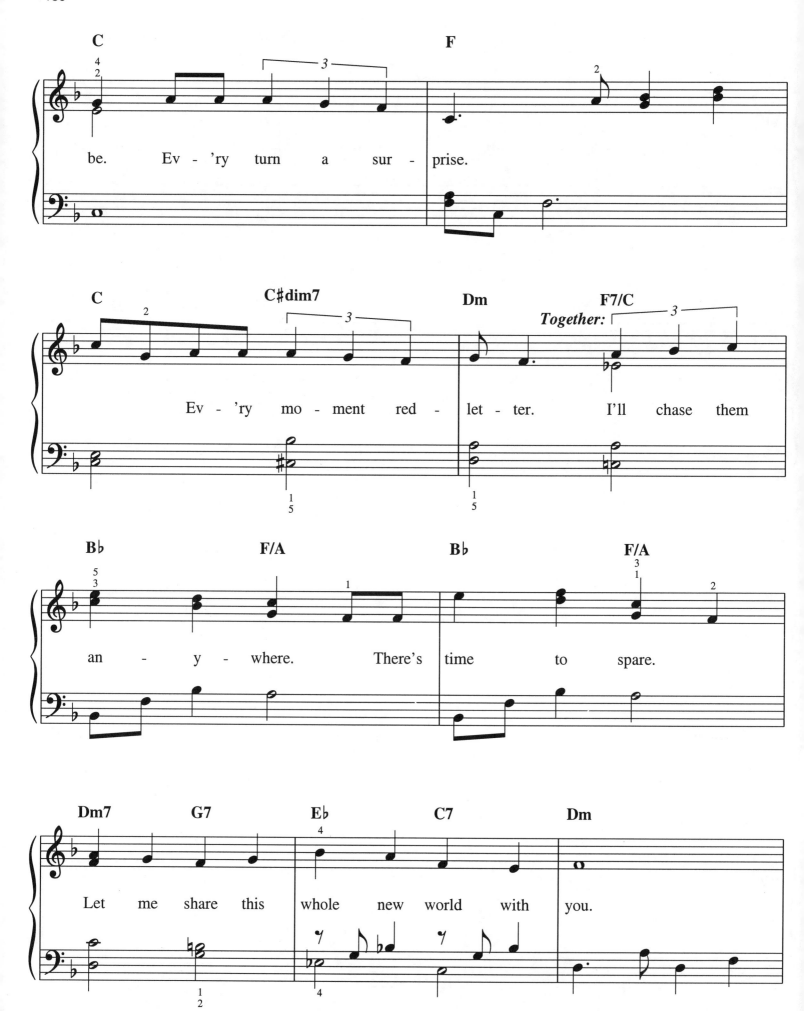

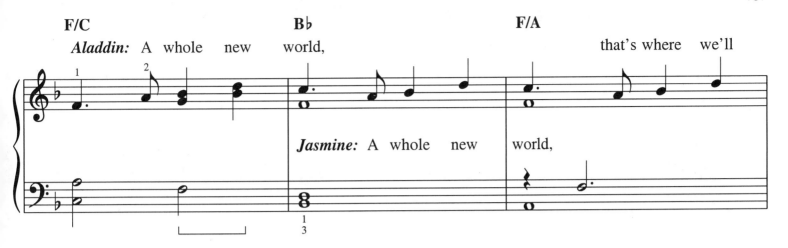

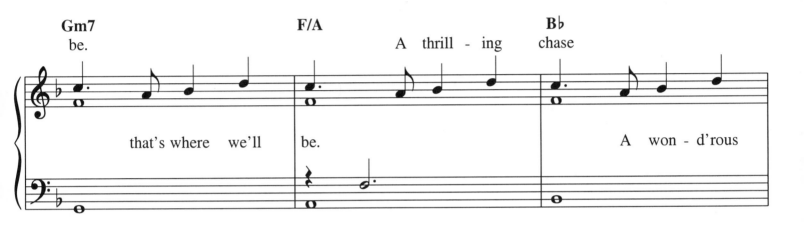

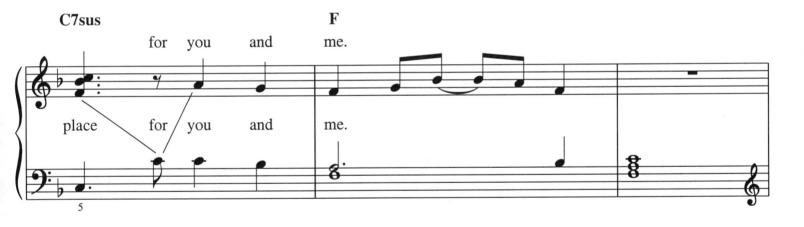

WHEN SHE LOVED ME

from Walt Disney Pictures' TOY STORY 2 - A Pixar Film

Music and Lyrics by
RANDY NEWMAN

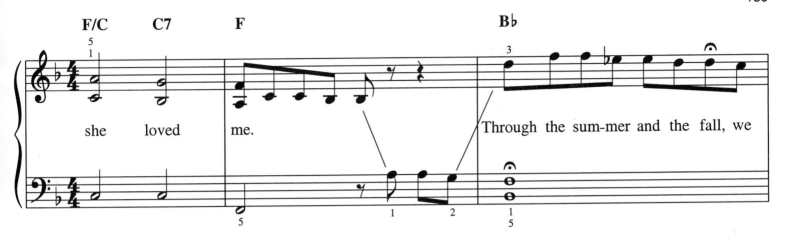

she   loved   me.   Through the sum-mer and the fall, we

had each oth-er, that was all. Just she and I to-geth-er, like it was meant to be.

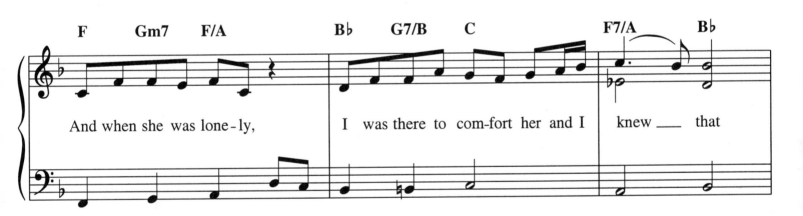

And when she was lone-ly, I was there to com-fort her and I knew ___ that

she   loved   me.

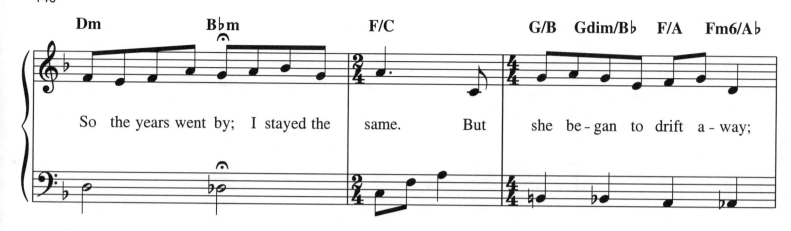

So the years went by; I stayed the same. But she be-gan to drift a-way;

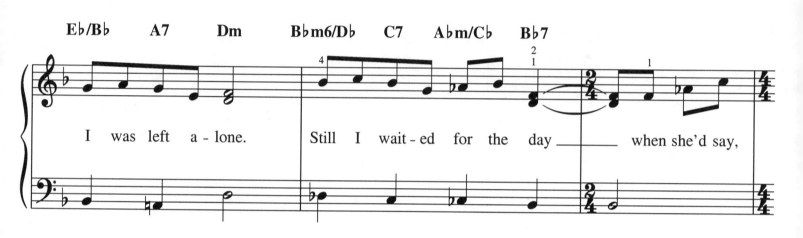

I was left a-lone. Still I wait-ed for the day _____ when she'd say,

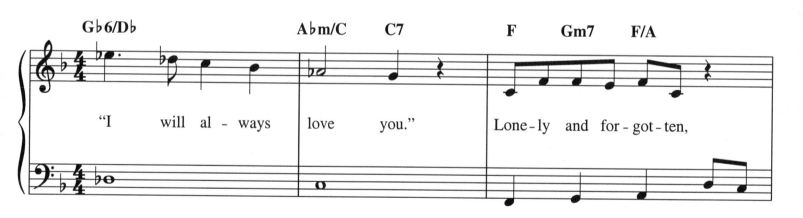

"I will al-ways love you." Lone-ly and for-got-ten,

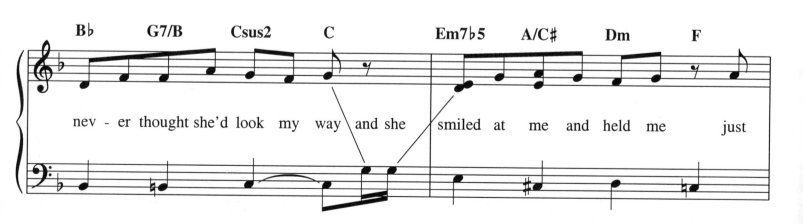

nev-er thought she'd look my way and she smiled at me and held me just

like she used to do   like she loved   me   when she

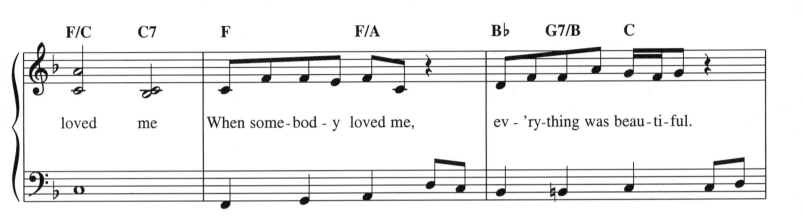

loved   me   When some-bod - y loved me,   ev - 'ry-thing was beau-ti-ful.

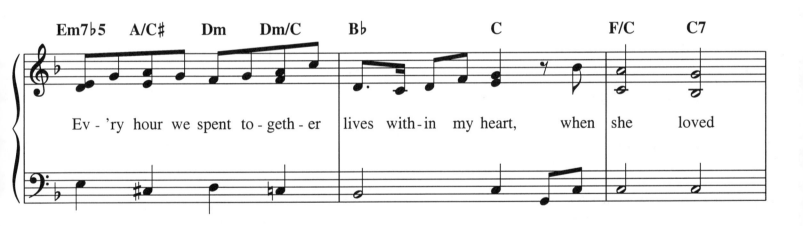

Ev - 'ry hour we spent to - geth - er   lives with-in my heart,   when she   loved

me.

WHEN YOU SAY NOTHING AT ALL

Words and Music by PAUL OVERSTREET
and DON SCHLITZ

Moderately slow

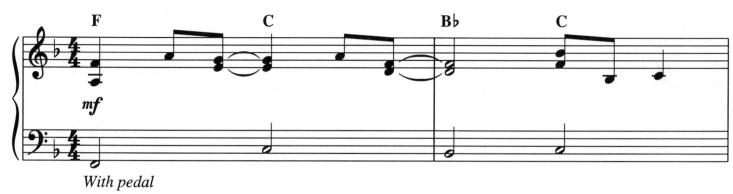

mf

With pedal

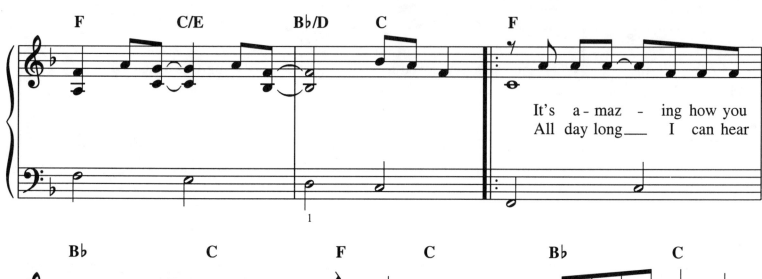

It's a-maz - ing how you
All day long___ I can hear

can speak right___ to my heart___
peo - ple talk - ing out loud.___

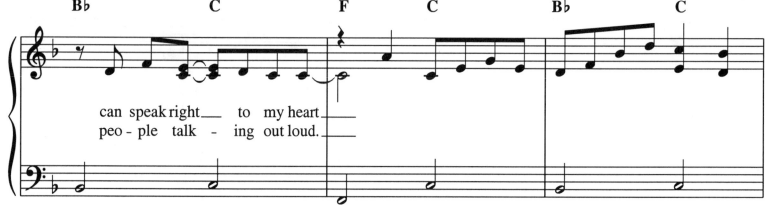

With - out say - ing a word___
But when you___ hold me near___

you can light up the dark.
you drown out the crowd.

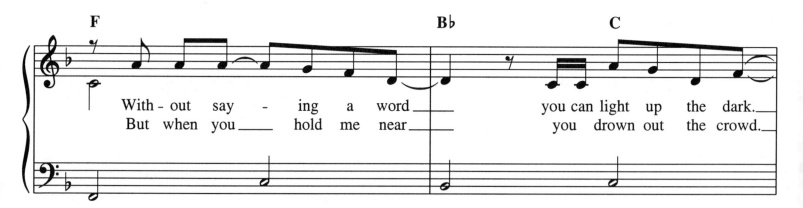

2.

when you say noth - ing at all.___

D.S. al Coda

The

CODA

when you say noth-ing at all.___

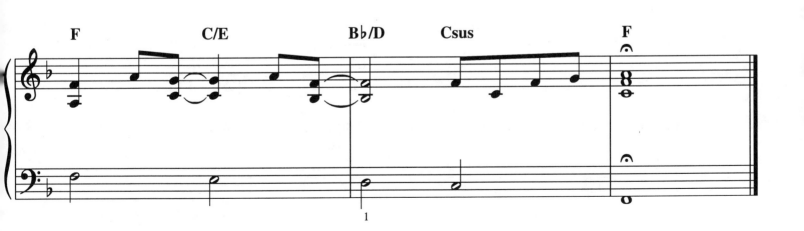

YOU'LL BE IN MY HEART

(Pop Version)
from Walt Disney Pictures' TARZAN™

Words and Music by
PHIL COLLINS